To Life!

Jewish Reflections on Everyday Living

For Sally —

with love and blessings
for a life of meaning.

To Life!

Az Fedma

Praise for
TO LIFE! JEWISH REFLECTIONS
ON EVERYDAY LIVING

"Amy Hirshberg Lederman is a teacher, writer and an insightful human being. All of these qualities come together in this collection of reflections on life. I thought a little, cried a little, laughed a little and enjoyed it all immensely!"

**Dr. Betsy Dolgin Katz, Director,
Florence Melton Adult Mini-School;
coauthor, *The Adult Jewish Education Handbook
(A.R.E. Publication)***

"Amy Hirshberg Lederman celebrates Jewish identity by finding meaning, purpose and belonging in the twist and flow of daily life. 'TO LIFE!' prompts us to pay closer attention to the sacred imbedded in the details of living."

**Rabbi Elie Kaplan Spitz, author,
*Does the Soul Survive? A Jewish Journey to Belief
in Afterlife, Past Lives, and Living with Purpose***

"Amy Hirshberg Lederman deftly defeats readers' defenses. She applies ancient Jewish traditions with a soft, unthreatening tenacity to contemporary quandaries, both personal and professional. Vulnerable and honest, Lederman allows the Torah to challenge and inform our life. 'To Life!' is warm, bracing and instructive. Enjoy!"

Rabbi Hillel Goldberg, PhD., author, *The Fire Within;* Executive Editor, *Intermountain Jewish News*

"Lederman's 'To Life!' captures the warmth and wisdom of Jewish culture in her uplifting tales of our shared experiences."

Dr. Leonard Dinnerstein, author, *The Leo Frank Case* and *Anti-Semitism in America*

"Amy Hirshberg Lederman writes from the Jewish heart and soul. 'To Life!' is a joy to read."

Mike Sirota, Editor, *San Diego Jewish Times*

To Life!

Jewish Reflections on Everyday Living

Amy Hirshberg Lederman

Published in the United States of America by:
ALIYAH PUBLISHING
5425 E. Broadway Blvd. PMB #242
Tucson AZ 85711-3704
Phone: 520-790-2879
Fax: (520) 207-0510
www.aliyahpublishing.com

Publication Date: 2005

Front cover artwork by Gail T. Roberts
© 2004, All rights reserved.

Back cover photograph by Marcia Gold

Book design by Patte Lazarus/GroundZero Design

Library of Congress Control Number: 2004097877

ISBN 0-9761456-0-X

Printed in the United States of America

"Surely this instruction that I give you this day is not too baffling for you, nor is it beyond reach. It is not in the heavens that you should say, "Who among us can go up to the heavens and get it for us and impart it to us, that we may observe it?" Neither is it beyond the sea, that you should say, "Who among us can cross to the other side of the sea and get it for us and impart it to us, that we may observe it?" No the thing is very close to you, in your mouth and in your heart, for you to observe it."

Deuteronomy: 30:11-14

To Life!

$\mathcal{I}$NTRODUCTION

$\mathcal{A}$s a Jewish teacher, I have heard my students express feelings of estrangement from Judaism, a confession which is often born from a sense of frustration or disappointment with the Judaism of their childhoods or, in some cases, from not having any Jewish childhood at all. They feel disconnected; unsure of the traditions for holidays, hesitant to follow rules they don't understand and uncertain if any of it is relevant to their lives. They want more from their Judaism but don't know how or where to begin.

Like many Jews I meet, I spent most of my youth doodling in Hebrew school and thinking of ways to get out of going to synagogue. While I relished my grandmother's chicken soup and the holidays we spent at her home when I was a child, I realized as a young adult that I, like my students, also lacked the knowledge and Jewish "know-how" to observe most rituals, traditions and holidays. Yet unlike other skills that I had not acquired, admitting to being "Jewishly disadvantaged" felt embarrassing and even shameful.

The path I traveled to come home to my Judaism has taken many twists and turns. As a teenager, I spent nights reading the New Testament at a local Christian coffee house, attended Christmas mass and Easter services with my boyfriend and studied with interfaith friends at Bahai firesides. My parents were naturally concerned (more about the boyfriend than the Easter services) but never stopped me from exploring what other religions had to say or offer.

In college I found true love when I met up with Jewish philosophers like Mendelsohn, Buber and Heschel; great Jewish thinkers who challenged me to reflect more, experience more and be more as a Jew. My thirst for Jewish knowledge became the catalyst which transported me across the sea to Israel for my junior year – a time that forever changed the way I view myself as a woman, a Jew and an American.

Since my first trip to Israel I have grown slowly but steadily into my Judaism like a well-worn overcoat. I have shaped its pockets with continuing questions, adjusted its collar to fit my changing needs as I have evolved from a backpacking college student to attorney, wife and mother. With each age and stage of my life I am able to understand Jewish wisdom and tradition in new ways and it is this evolving appreciation that keeps it vital and meaningful for me. Over the years, I have learned Hebrew, studied classical Jewish texts, tried my hand at Jewish meditation. In my efforts to learn more, I have grappled not only with the meaning of the texts but with the meaning of life itself.

At the core of Jewish wisdom is a profound understanding of human nature, an awareness of how our strengths and vulnerabilities affect our actions and relationships. Digging deep into my Judaism has enabled me to find meaning in the everyday things I do and the relationships I have. It has helped me live with intention and clarity of purpose which enables me to be more grounded as a daughter, wife, sister, mother and friend. Simply put, Jewish wisdom has helped me in my struggle to become a better, more complete person.

The Jewish answer to the question "where do I start?" is this: Right here and right now. At whatever point you are in your life, with whatever level of knowledge you have, at whatever level of commitment you feel. Regardless of age, occupation, experience or background, it is not so important *where* you begin but *that* you begin.

In my own search to discover Judaism, I started by reading the primary Jewish text. The Torah (also called the Five Books of Moses) is the bedrock of Jewish thought and theology and is filled with stories about the Jewish people's encounter with God. However we understand the Torah, whether we believe it is the Divine Revelation of God or the inspired writings of man, it represents the Jewish blueprint for living which has guided Jews throughout history.

My continuing need to question and understand the words of the Torah led me to study the teachings of the Talmudic rabbis who discussed and debated the meaning of the Torah as they struggled to understand it over two thousand years ago. Filled with legal rulings, legends, homilies and parables, it is like a continuous conversation over 400 years between the best and brightest minds of the times. Despite the enormous differences between their lives and mine, I have found that they were not so different from many people I know. For at the heart of their efforts, was the struggle to live a meaningful life in a tumultuous and uncertain world.

To Life! Jewish Reflections on Everyday Living is the result of my own search to live a more meaningful life as a person and a Jew. It is an invitation to look at life through a Jewish lens, to see how Judaism can imbue it with wisdom, compassion, humor and purpose. It speaks about matters of the heart: about family, feelings, money, friends, work, holidays, education, loss and death. It is not intended as a "how-to-be-Jewish" book; it is offered as a framework through which to view what you do in your carpool, kitchen or office as uniquely Jewish because everything you do and are has the potential for holiness.

The pages that follow are filled with personal stories and essays, many of which have found their home in a column I write which is published in a number of Jewish newspapers across the United States. Some stories are humorous; others are sad, challenging or provocative. All are written with a deep and abiding love and respect for the Jewish rabbis, sages and texts that have provided guidance and wisdom throughout Jewish history and who have become my teachers as well. It is my deepest hope that they will fill your heart, mind and home with a new appreciation for the treasury of Jewish wisdom that is the sacred inheritance of the Jewish people and the world.

I owe thanks and lots of hugs to the many people who have helped me on my journey from lawyer to Jewish educator to writer.

To my Jewish teachers and mentors, especially Rabbi Andre Ungar, Rabbi Israel and Esther Becker, Rabbi Thomas Louchheim, Dr. Byron Sherwin, Dr. Betsy Dolgin Katz, Rabbi Levi Kellman, Rabbi Elie Kaplan Spitz and the many wonderful CLAL teachers I have known over the years, a heartfelt *todah rabbah*.

To the many professional mentors in the Tucson Jewish community who have guided (and nudged) me along the way, including Stuart Mellan, Carol Karsch, Myrna Lyons and Barbara Chandler, you are the best.

To the Arizona Jewish Post, especially Editors Sandy Heiman and Phyllis Braun, I owe you a continuing debt of gratitude for taking a chance on my writing.

To my dear friends Gail Roberts, Brenna Lacey, Bari Ross, Linda Newmark and Robin Baade, thank you for the countless hours of edits of my half-baked stories.

To my very first writing group, Nan Rubin, Jacqueline Bland and Ida Plotkin, without whom my courage would have sunk to the bottom of my coffee cup, thank you for always being honest.

To my devoted friend, critic and legal counselor, Robert Fortuno, thank you for continually keeping me informed and out of trouble.

To my parents, Elise and Hal Hirshberg, who still can't figure out why a nice Jewish girl from New Jersey would give up her law career to do this, and to my brother Jeff who taught me the meaning of integrity and honor, thanks for all your love and support.

To my wonderful children, Joshua and Lauren, who have been my most scrutinizing editors and critics, in your love I am doubly blessed.

And last but never least to my soul mate, teacher and dearest friend Ray, without whom I would never have had the opportunity, audacity or confidence to write this book, I love you always.

TO LIFE!

CONTENTS

BEING HUMAN

FAMILY

HOLIDAYS

THE EVERYDAY ORDINARY

GROWING AND LEARNING

MATTERS OF LIFE AND DEATH

TO LIFE!

BEING HUMAN

THE GOOD, THE BAD AND THE HUMAN

I was five the year my brother became a Bar Mitzvah and it was the worst year of my life. For approximately six months preceding the Big Event, he was fussed over, shopped for, listened to and pumped up while I was relegated to the back burner of family life. One evening during dinner I took matters into my own hands and kicked him so hard under the table that he dropped the platter of chicken and potatoes, splattering our meal in every direction but the plates. The results were disastrous: my mother became hysterical, I was sent to my room without supper and my brother got even more attention.

Stunned by my behavior, my parents demanded to know why I kicked my brother. My answer was immediate and unwavering: "I didn't do it."

They were aghast. Not only had I misbehaved big time, but my naughtiness had sunk to an even lower level of bold-faced lying. "What do you mean you didn't do it?" my father asked incredulously.

"I didn't do it!" I cried emphatically." "BAD Amy did it!"

In my youthful mind, it was a simple as this: I played no part in the dinner disaster because I was a *good* girl. It was BAD Amy, the other girl who lived inside me, that had kicked my brother.

My five-year-old answer was a very natural and human response to disconnect the "bad" parts of myself from the good ones. GOOD Amy would never kick her brother because that would mean that she was a nasty, hostile and worst of all, BAD girl.

When it comes to being good or bad, the rabbis of the Talmud talked about it as much as Freud, Oprah and Dr. Laura combined. They acknowledged that we are born with both good and evil instincts, but only acquire a need to be good as we mature. In somewhat confusing and paradoxical language, they described the human instinct-for-bad as the inner force that drives us to be good. Sounds like rabbinic brain teaser? In some ways it is.

The key to this riddle is found in the rabbinic interpretation of the word "instinct" (or *Yetzer* in Hebrew). The rabbis construed instinct to mean certain innate, essential drives, urges, or impulses that form the basis of the human soul. We are born with the "instinct" – for both good and bad. The instinct-for-good is what makes us want to uphold God's will and laws by performing deeds of justice, compassion and righteousness. The instinct-for-bad is what drives us to promote our own well-being and strive for personal achievement and success. Both are deeply human and both are necessary for the physical and spiritual survival and perpetuation of humankind.

The Talmud teaches that the desire for sex stems from our instinct-for-bad; without it, we would not build a house, marry, have children or conduct a business. It is the sexual drive that makes us want to create and affirm life; it motivates us to fill the earth and establish our homes, our livelihoods and our communities.

The Talmud also teaches that "the greater the man, the greater his evil inclination." Our human potential for greatness, our capacity to develop and generate new ideas and our ability to lead others are all linked to our sexual vitality (similar to Freud's theory linking the libido to human creativity).

Why is the instinct-for-bad considered evil if it motivates us to do good? Because the energy that underlies our drive to create, run a business and establish ourselves on earth can, in the extreme, become the source of our over-ambitiousness, excessive competitiveness, self interest and disregard for the welfare of others.

The key is how we *use* our instinct-for-bad: When we harness, moderate and redirect our impulses to lie, cheat, steal, hurt others or disobey God's law, we elevate ourselves above the animals to become more human and more humane. In essence, how we use or refrain from using the bad in us is what enables us to be good as well as human.

Many years have passed since I first renounced my instinct-for-bad. To be honest, there are still times in my adult life that I wish I could sever the "bad" parts of myself from the good. It is comforting to know that Judaism does not expect me to be only good. Rather, it acknowledges that we are human beings *because* we have both good and bad within us. It is the way we master the instincts we possess that makes us who we are.

Judging Others with Compassion

About a month after 9/11, I had to give a speech in Pittsburgh. As I waited to board the plane, I noticed a very burly, foreign-looking man with more body piercings than a pin cushion get in line behind me. My first thought was to change planes before this "would-be terrorist" had a chance to blow it up. Not wanting to overreact however, I forced myself to get on the plane and ordered a Bloody Mary with breakfast.

When we landed safely in Pittsburgh, I watched the terrorist get off, wondering if he would be greeted by a group of thugs wearing leather jackets and dark glasses. What I saw sent a shock through my system, reminding me just how unfair and unkind my judgments can be. The group that met this man was none other than his three, adorable children and a wife who couldn't wait to hand over the fourth – an infant no more than six weeks old. "Hugs, not thugs," I thought sheepishly as I marched off to baggage claim.

I know, I know. "It's natural," you say. "We all judge others sometimes, on the basis of how they look, what they wear, how they speak, how they spend their time and money." But while it may be a natural and human tendency to judge others, the question still remains: Is it right?

Jewish tradition has much to say about how we judge others. Leviticus 19: 15 states that "with righteousness shall you judge your fellow." This has been interpreted as requiring us to give others the benefit of the doubt when evaluating their behavior, to view them through a lens of compassion, understanding and kindness. Great advice which is easier said than done. For while I might be able to make excuses for why someone mistreats his employees, is rude at a party, or never gives to charity, my negative judgments will most likely affect my feelings for him regardless of the justifications I make for his behavior.

The Talmud provides a practical insight into this matter in Ethics of the Fathers 1:6 where we are told to "Judge everyone favorably." A proper Hebrew translation is actually "Judge the whole of a person favorably." Jewish tradition acknowledges that we are born with the capacity for both good and bad. Rather than evaluating a person based on the things we disapprove of or dislike in him, we are taught to look at the entire person in his wholeness before making judgments. We are asked to take into account the complexities of being human; to acknowledge the good and bad qualities, the kindheartedness as well as the thoughtlessness, the loving words as well as the hurtful ones, in order to remain open and fair in the ultimate conclusions we draw about another human being.

The Talmud also reminds us to be cautious in rendering a decision. Not something I did when I wrongly assessed my would-be terrorist or others whom I have unfairly judged simply because I did not know them or was uncomfortable or unfamiliar with the way they spoke, dressed or behaved.

Jewish tradition wisely recognizes the human tendency to pass judgment on others without fully understanding the cultural background, mental or physical challenges, psychological or financial stresses or inner feelings that motivate a person to act. That is why the sagely words of Rabbi Hillel spoken almost two thousand years ago still ring true today: "Do not judge another person until you have reached his place."

"That's Not Fair!" –
What's Jewish About Protest

"*T*hat's not fair! She got more than I did! You love him more than me!" How many times have you heard those plaintive words from a small child? How many times have you thought them yourself as an adult?

From the earliest of years, we are born protesters. While many of our protests are based on subjective feelings and emotions rather than verifiable truths, it doesn't change the fact that when something doesn't feel right or fair, human nature calls upon us to respond.

The Jewish people come from a long line of protesters. The granddaddy of them all emerges in the Book of Genesis when Abraham confronts God about His decision to destroy the inhabitants of Sodom and Gomorrah. Abraham demands that God explain the moral reasoning of His decision and boldly protests against it in a moving passage that is described by the Jewish philosopher, Emil Fackenheim, as an incident of "citing God against God."

With moxie and defiance, Abraham challenges God with this question: "Will you sweep away the righteous with the wicked? Shall not the Judge of all the earth do justice?" (Genesis 18:17-26) Abraham's protest sets the standard for future moral awareness and establishes the precedent that the right to challenge unjust orders is actually tied to a mandate to do so.

Jewish history is replete with examples of Jewish men and women who defied leaders and laws when they violated moral conscience. Moses challenged Pharoah and demanded that he free the Jewish slaves from Egyptian bondage so that they could serve God. A less known but equally inspiring story is found in the opening chapter of Exodus where the Hebrew midwives, Shifrah and Puah, disobeyed Pharaoh's order to kill all Hebrew newborn boys using the pretext that the babies were born before the mid-wives arrived. From Abraham to Rabbi Akiva, from Supreme Court Justice Louis Brandeis to Soviet dissident Natan Sharansky, Jews throughout history have protested vehemently against immoral and unconscionable laws. The Talmud, that sacred Jewish text which interprets the Torah, states our obligation to protest as follows: "If a person can protest the misdeeds of his household, yet does not, he becomes guilty with them. If he can protest the deeds of his townsmen, and does not, he is guilty with them. If he can protest the deeds of the entire world, and does not, he is guilty with them." (Shabbat 54b)

When I first read this quote I felt overwhelmed. I already spend too much time feeling guilty about little things like not calling my mother enough or forgetting my brother's birthday. I don't need to feel guilty about not protesting every moral wrong I read about in the paper or hear on the news. Or do I?

Judaism recognizes that the ability to protest is not the same for everyone. Some of us are limited by our physical abilities, others by financial constraints. But what is essential to the idea is that each one of us has the capacity, no matter how great or how small, to stand up to injustice when we see it.

According to traditional Jewish law, the epicenter of our obligation is found where we live, in our homes. Our primary duty is to protest against the inequities that reside within our own four walls. We can respond to this obligation in positive and affirming ways through "family meetings" where domestic issues like bedtime, computer use, sibling rivalry or curfew are openly discussed. We can build healthier marriages by expressing feelings of inequity or resentment before they fester and become toxic to the relationship. We can teach our children to stand up for what they believe is right, whether it is friend who is teased by the class bully or the right for gays to marry. Regardless of the magnitude of the gesture, it remains our individual responsibility to protest when things are not fair in our homes. Beyond that, we are charged to look into our community and then ultimately, out into the world.

While it is true that not everyone has the *direct* capacity to affect change through protest, we all have the ability, however small it may seem, and the obligation to do so. How much better a place the world will be when we respond to the call.

LASHON HARA: WALK THE WALK
BUT DON'T TALK THE TALK

J have a confession to make. Last week I committed a crime of the worst sort and got busted. No, I didn't steal makeup from Wal-Mart, run a red light or cheat on my taxes. But according to the rabbis of the Talmud, what I did was tantamount to murder or idolatry.

It began innocently enough one afternoon when I wrote an email to a friend about a surprise birthday party we were planning for a mutual friend. In her response she asked if we should invite a specific person and I wrote back as follows:

"We can invite her if you want but she's such a downer, always complaining about things. The last time I went to dinner with her, she sent the meal back three times. Do you really think she should come?"

I sent the email back without giving it a second thought. But instead of sending it back to my friend, I sent it by mistake to a group email address in which the woman I wrote about was included. I had no idea of this awful mix-up until the next morning when I received an email from the woman which simply inquired: Is what you wrote about me *lashon hara?*

I wanted to crawl into a hole and die.

The concept of lashon hara (literally "evil tongue" in Hebrew) means the making of derogatory or damaging remarks about someone that might cause him or her physical, psychological or economic harm, even if the remark is true. The remark can be communicated in any number of ways, such as in person, on the phone, in writing or in my case, in cyberspace. Unlike the American laws regarding libel and slander which prohibit the making of untrue statements about a third party, lashon hara goes one step further and prohibits statements that are negative but true. Even if the listener/reader already knows about the

information from other sources, we are commanded not to
repeat it.

Through our words we have the power to create,
communicate, enlighten, heal and love; we also have the
power to impair, diminish, denigrate, humiliate and
destroy. Yet most of us take more time in choosing the
clothes we wear, the food we eat and the movies we watch
than in choosing the words we use every day when speaking to or about our children, parents, co-workers, teachers
and friends. And while I'm not a betting woman, I would
wager that one of the least observed commandments in the
Torah is the prohibition: "Do not go about as a talebearer
among your fellows." (Leviticus 19:16)

The rabbis of the Talmud compare the act of gossip to
murder because it kills three people: the person who says it,
the person who listens to it and the person about whom it
is said. (Arakhin 15b) There are exceptions to the rule however. If the person to whom you are speaking needs the
information because he or she is contemplating marriage
with the person, hiring, or going into business with him or
her, then it is considered appropriate to communicate
information that might affect that particular decision.

What I learned through my own failings is an essential
life lesson. *Lashon Hara* is anything that I communicate to
someone about someone else (even if its true) that I will feel
badly about if the person about whom I am speaking finds
out. It is not a difficult concept to understand but it is a
hard one to observe.

TO ERR IS HUMAN: TO FORGIVE, NEARLY IMPOSSIBLE

*T*he year my daughter Lauren became a Bat Mitzvah, she gave me a gift I will never forget. She taught me how to forgive.

Anna and I were more than sisters, better than best friends. We were the closest of confidantes all through college. I was the maid-of-honor at her wedding. She stayed at my apartment when things got tough at home.

Perhaps I should have detected the early warning signs of a friendship going bad. But since I wasn't inclined to doubt Anna's motives, I justified her actions even when they hurt my feelings. Like the night she forgot about my surprise birthday party because she was with her boyfriend. Or the time I was in New York City for a visit but she barely made time to see me.

We both wanted children desperately and I was the first one to have a baby. She promised to come for a visit, to see the baby and help me out. I was so in love with my new son that as the days passed into weeks, I barely noticed she hadn't called or written. Then I went back to work.

It was hard to accept that she hadn't contacted me during those first few months. By the time my son started crawling, I knew she never would. That's when I picked up the phone and confronted her.

"Why haven't you called me?" I practically screamed into the phone. "Why haven't you come to see the baby?"

Her answer cut me to the core.

"I just don't want to get into it right now. I have a lot going on at work and can't deal with us or our relationship."

The phone went dead and so did my heart. I knew the friendship was over.

For more than 15 years I tried to find a way to forgive her, to make some sense out of what she did to me. No matter how hard I tried or how much I prayed, I couldn't let go of the pain. I talked about it with my friends, my family, my therapist, but nothing I did made me feel any better.

Then my daughter confronted me about a week before her Bat Mitzvah.

"You should just call her up, you know," she started the conversation mid-thought.

"Who?" I asked, thinking she meant a cousin or aunt who hadn't sent back the r.s.v.p card yet.

"Anna, your used-to-be-best-friend. You should just call her up and ask her what happened. Why she was so mean to you. Maybe she was in trouble, or really sad or confused and couldn't talk about it then and now she feels sorry."

I shook my head. "No way, honey. That's over and done with. If my friendship meant anything to her, she would have called me up years ago to explain."

"Well, I still think you should do it. You keep feeling bad and it won't go away until you do something."

Sage advice from my not-yet-thirteen year old, which, after much hesitation, I decided to follow. With trembling hands, I dialed Anna's number and took a deep breath when I heard her voice. As best as I could, I told her that I wanted to resolve what had happened between us so many years ago.

Less than three days later I received a letter in the mail, in which Anna poured her heart out and told me things I never knew were going on in her life. She asked for my forgiveness and pleaded with me to understand why she had been unable to talk about it all these years.

It seems that my daughter intuitively understood a very Jewish concept: that when someone hurts you, you should try to find ways to forgive. But letting go – of past hurts, injuries and wrongs is one of the hardest life lessons to learn.

Jewish tradition teaches that when someone hurts you – physically, emotionally or financially, he is required to ask you for forgiveness. If not, then even God cannot forgive him. But when he sincerely asks for forgiveness, Jewish law wants you to forgive and to do it wholeheartedly.

Most of us have experienced the emotional reward that accompanies the act of forgiveness. Letting go of hurt feelings frees up the energy we use to stay angry at the people who have wounded us. That energy is then able to be used to generate more positive things in our life which can enrich and enhance our happiness, communication, success and even love.

Judaism promises a spiritual reward when we forgive others as well. We are taught that if we show compassion to those who offend us, then God will show us the same compassion when we offend Him.

Our sages succinctly summed it up when they answered the question "Whose sin is forgiven?" as follows: "The sin of one who forgives sins committed against him (or herself) is forgiven." (Megillah 28a)

The Gift of Giving

I have been accused my entire life by everyone I know of exaggerating. But it's no exaggeration when I tell you that I was *literally* walking out the door to a photo shoot for a new headshot when the phone rang and a woman to whom I had never spoken before opened the conversation with these words:

"Hi. I'm a photographer and I love reading your columns but I hate that picture of you with those bugged-out eyes that make you look like you're in shock." Speaking of shock, I could barely move my mouth fast enough to ask, "And to whom am I speaking?"

In a good-natured way, Marcia told me that she was a professional photographer and a voice teacher who had moved to Tucson many years ago. She offered to take my picture for free, just to give me the opportunity to have a better and more current picture of myself. I hesitated for the moment it took me to swallow my pride and then set the date for the following week, thinking that this is what my father meant when he said: "Never look a gift horse in the mouth."

Marcia arrived with rolls of film, several cameras and a flurry of energy. She evaluated my patio and yard like a real estate agent, finding photographic value in natural and reflective light that I couldn't even detect. I sat for more than an hour, tilting my head one way, moving my shoulder another, fearing all the while that my laugh lines would look far worse in the outdoor light than the professional studio I had cancelled my appointment with.

But over the course of that hour, she told me wonderful stories about her life, stopping to point out a beautiful shadow or flower that formed the backdrop to my headshot. Her words and mannerism helped me relax and become more natural in front of the camera. She had a true gift; she could impart her vision of beauty and light with a genuineness that melted away all self-consciousness. I became so absorbed in watching her work that by the time she finished the roll, I was so calm I could have taken a nap. We all enter this world with distinctive biological, physical and spiritual traits. Our natural skills and talents as well as those we intentionally develop become an essential part of the currency we use in the marketplace of life. So why is it that so many of us don't recognize our own gifts? And what is it about the act of giving that helps us appreciate ourselves and others differently?

The Jewish sages spent many years grappling with the essence of our humanity. They tell us that we are all equal because we originated from the same man, Adam. They emphasize our uniqueness when they remind us that God made us in the form of the first human being but that no person is comparable to any other. They affirm our infinite worth when they proclaim that whoever destroys or saves a single soul is like one who destroys or saves the entire world. (Sanhedrin 4:5) In a period of history when therapy was unheard of, the rabbis took the lead in delivering a message of positive esteem: that as human beings we are to treasure the fact that we are unique, infinitely valuable and equal in worth.

The act of giving enables us to become more aware of ourselves and others. It helps us recognize our own special abilities by translating them into concrete, tangible resources. It lets us appreciate what we have and makes us more aware of the needs of others. And it gives us a chance to offer the best part of ourselves hoping that we will enable others to live a better, more comfortable or more meaningful life.

So why don't more of us pick up the phone and offer to help someone we think might benefit from a skill or service we have? Perhaps it's because many of us feel that we have nothing special to offer, no amazing talents or creative gifts.

Perhaps we believe that our skills are not important enough or that our abilities fall short of others who seem to be more talented or competent than we are. Or maybe we are afraid to put ourselves on the line by offering our time or help.

Jewish wisdom has long understood this basic human insecurity of not "being enough" or "having enough" to be able to give. That is why the Talmud assures us that: "To the one who is eager to give, God provides the means." (Bava Batra 9b)

I'll admit that at first it was hard to learn that my old headshot was less than terrific in the eyes of one of my readers. But when I look at my new headshot, I am reminded of the bold and generous stranger who offered to share her time and talent with me simply because she had a gift to give. I can only imagine that if each one of us made the effort to give to someone else a gift like Marcia gave to me, the world would be a far richer place and we would be no poorer for the giving.

$\mathcal{F}$AMILY

CHICKEN SOUP AND CANDLESTICKS: RITUALS CREATE SECURITY FOR OUR FAMILIES

$\mathcal{M}$y husband and I don't always agree on things. When it comes to family matters, we have fought over everything from cloth versus paper diapers to whether M and M's constitute one of the four food groups. The one thing we do agree upon, however, is that our home should be a safe haven for our children; a place where they can take risks as they grow, express opinions without fear and learn to understand the challenge inherent in loving and living with others.

How my husband and I create a safe environment is by very different means. He locks the doors and windows; I sit on the couch and invite conversation. He wants a dog, an alarm system and to know where the kids are at all times; I want to cook a big pot of soup and have dinner together. Neither one is complete without the other and together we have created our own gourmet blend of physical and emotional security that works.

Despite our differences, there is a particular tool we both rely upon in creating a safe family environment. Ritual, that age-old vehicle which societies have used for centuries

to transmit values to its members, has done more to help
build our family than almost anything else.

Sociologists and anthropologists have long known that
rituals function as powerful tools to define family roles and
to pass on cultural norms and family values from one
generation to the next. Rituals create a sense of identity and
belonging; they tie the individual to a group or community.
They mark important life-cycle events, commemorate life
transitions and permit us to express important emotions
such as love, fear, joy and grief. Perhaps most importantly,
rituals provide us with a sense of stability, order and
regularity: They constitute an anchor in a tumultuous
world and act as a compass by which to navigate.

When I was growing up my family did not observe
many Jewish rituals. We did not celebrate Shabbat or keep
Kosher. None of us knew which prayers were said for eating,
drinking, or celebrating the holidays. As a child it didn't
matter much but as an adult it felt like a huge impediment.
I sheepishly muddled my way through Jewish events and
services feeling culturally disadvantaged and downright
stupid. Then one day I read about Rabbi Akiva, one of the
most highly acclaimed Jewish sages, who began his Jewish
studies at the age of forty. Since I was in my early twenties
at the time, this left me feeling as if I had a definite advantage. I stopped worrying about what I didn't know and
began a course of Jewish learning that continues to this day.

My own definition of ritual is quite simple: It is the
creation of sacred time or sacred space in our lives, our
home, and our community. In our home it has taken many
forms and has evolved through the years as we have grown
up as a family together. It speaks to us in our kitchen where
we are daily reminded of the commitment we make to our
tradition as we place the turkey burgers on our "meat only"
plates. It carries its force into our family room, where we
have shelves dedicated solely to Jewish collectables, art,
music and books, many of which have special meaning or

were made by our children. It makes its way into our bedrooms where we have hung a mezuzah on each door that contains personal blessings and prayers for our family. Each week as we usher in Shabbat, we whisper something special to each of our teenage children acknowledging their uniqueness and why we love them. Years ago this time was allocated to "happy thoughts", when our children would share the happiest moments of the week with us. We light my grandmother's brass candlesticks, smuggled out of Russia over 100 years ago in the lining of a coat, while my daughter wears her black lace head covering that still smells of Grandma's rosewater cologne.

We find new ways to celebrate the holidays using art, music, food and games. On Rosh HaShanah, we bake a birthday cake for dessert to honor the world's birthday. On Passover, we sit on pillows and blankets in a tent we build on our back porch to experience the Seder as if in Egypt. When it is time to eat, we exit the tent and walk the long distance through our sandy back yard "to the Promised Land" for dinner. The opportunities to create meaningful rituals are unlimited if you are willing to spend some time doing a little background reading and experimenting with your family.

Making our homes a safe harbor for our children is no easy undertaking. I am grateful for what Judaism has to offer us as individuals and parents as we continue to embrace the challenge.

The Day My Mother
Stopped Playing God

"My dear friend Helene died last week," my mother informed me sadly as if consoling us both. "I'll miss her terribly. She really changed my life and the way I viewed the world."

I turned and looked into my mother's face, aged not so much by years as by the losses and disappointments she has endured. She is not prone to 'waxing philosophical' so her statement intrigued me.

"What do you mean, mom?" I asked, quietly taking her hand.

"Do you remember when you told me that you and Ray were planning to get married?"

I nodded, recalling the conversation with great discomfort. My mother tends to lead with her anxiety, and this conversation was no different. Her primary concern was not, as you might imagine, about his emotional commitment to me or his prospective financial stability. It was about his health.

"I think you should reconsider," she cautioned me at the time. "A man with diabetes may not live a long time, and you could end up a widow with children to raise on your own. Or what if he gets sick and you have to take care of him? It could ruin your life."

Dagger words which punctured my heart with their fatalism even though Ray was in great health at the time. But considering that her own father died from diabetes when she was just two years old, understandable.

"I'm willing to take the risk," I told her emphatically. "I may only have five weeks or five months or five years with him Mom, but it would be more than most people have in a lifetime."

My mother's voice brought me out of my reverie. She continued with her story.

"I told Helene about my fears and all the problems I imagined you would face if you two got married. And do you know what she told me? She looked me straight in the eyes and said: "Elise, STOP PLAYING GOD."

I have thought a lot about what my mother said, about my own tendencies to believe that if I worry enough, care enough, intervene enough, micro-manage enough I can ultimately control the events not only in my own life but in the lives of others, especially my children. As if by sheer will, desire and a sense of what *should* happen, I can determine the outcome and change the way life will inevitably unfold.

The Jewish antidote to our anxiety about the future is a five letter word called FAITH. Rabbi Menachem Mendel of Kotsk once said that: "Faith is clearer than sight." His words remind us that while human wisdom and understanding may not be sufficient to enable us to understand both the mysteries and tragedies of life, faith can provide the basis for belief in an inherent, holy order to the world. Faith is sensitivity to what transcends nature, knowledge and will; it is an awareness of the wholeness of life and of the holiness of life.

Maimonides, a great medieval Jewish scholar and physician, wrote from personal experience about our inability to know what the future may bring. In his early thirties, his brother David tragically drowned on a ship which went down with the family fortune, leaving Maimonides destitute. His words, although seemingly scientific, are written by a man whose belief in God makes all things possible.

"...Whatever a man fears may happen to him is only a matter of probability – either it will happen or it will not happen. And just as it is possible that something painful, worrisome and fearful may happen, it is also possible that, because of his reliance on God, the reverse of what he feared may happen. Because both, what he feared and the reverse, are possible."

My husband and I celebrated our 21st anniversary by spending a week hiking through Glacier National Park. He is as healthy as a horse and works hard to stay that way. I remind myself of that sagely advice from the Talmud whenever I begin to feel some of my mother's fears about the future coming on: "Do not worry about tomorrow's trouble, for you do not know what today may bring."

JEWISH SOUL MATES:
IS THIS MARRIAGE MADE IN HEAVEN?

*T*he night I met my husband was a warm evening in April and the smell of orange blossoms permeated the air. The date was "arranged" by mutual friends but I had lots of doubts about meeting their old college friend, a nice Jewish doctor from Los Angeles.

"If he's such a great guy, why is he 31 years old and not married?" I asked myself as I pulled into the parking lot, totally missing the irony of my own unmarried situation.

I knew, even before the chips and salsa arrived, that my children would have his eyes. Deep, calm, caring eyes that had me convinced in less than a minute that I had come home to the place I had been traveling 27 years to find.

I didn't know what it was called at the time but according to Jewish tradition, I had found my *bashert*, my true soul mate.

What is a soul mate? Is it a New Age concept to define true love? Is it a catchy phrase used by Romance novelists and publishers to sell books? Or does is mean something deeper and more essential, a spiritual bond between two people that is essential to fulfilling our heart's destiny?

The Bible gives us a glimpse of the origins of a soul mate in Genesis when God said: "It is not *good* for man to be alone; I will make him a helper corresponding to him." Loneliness is God's first concern about us as human beings. There is a sense that we will not be happy alone; that we need to be connected to another human being to experience companionship, support and the struggles inherent in a relationship if we are to achieve personal fulfillment and reach our highest potential. Adam, the first man, may have been complete in his physical being but without someone to love, without a partner with whom to relate, he was spiritually and emotionally incomplete.

In the story of Isaac and Rebekkah, we watch as Divine guidance directs the meeting of two people destined for one another when Abraham's servant Eliazar prays to God for a sign. Eliazar barely finishes his entreaty when Rebekkah appears and provides the exact sign that Eliazar has prayed for: she offers him and his camels water to drink. This is seen as more than a lucky coincidence; it is viewed as an act of Divine providence guiding Isaac to his true love.

The idea that heaven plays a part in the destiny of our hearts also appears in the Talmud, which describes a soul mate as someone who is chosen for us even before we are born. "Forty days before a child is born, a voice from heaven announces: 'The daughter of this person is destined for so-and-so.'" (Sotah 2a)

How do we find our soul mate? Jewish history provides us with several answers. Abraham's servant Eliazar is our first example of a Jewish matchmaker, a man on a mission to find the right wife for Isaac. During the twelfth century in Europe and Asia, it became customary to hire an intermediary (called a *Shadchan* in Hebrew) to find a suitable marriage partner. While this custom is no longer widely practiced, it is still followed in traditional Orthodox Jewish communities today.

Another answer has emerged from the world of technology. Jewish matchmaking in cyberspace is now a vibrant industry consisting of numerous websites offering successful matchmaking services for Jewish singles.

Not finding one's soul mate does not mean that one will live a loveless life. There are many forms of love and many types of loving relationships which nourish the heart and elevate the soul. Although different from a soul mate, a soulful relationship is one born out of true knowledge, caring, respect and love for another person which imbues life with emotional and spiritual meaning and purpose. Soulful relationships can occur throughout our lives with friends, co-workers, respected teachers, and family members as well as in our efforts to know and love God. In all cases, it is through our search for love and the belief and faith that we will find it, that we open ourselves up to finding soulful relationships as well as our true *bashert*.

My husband and I will celebrate our twenty-second wedding anniversary this year. While some may view ours as a "marriage made in heaven", we both know how hard we have struggled, worked, negotiated and compromised to make it a strong and loving relationship here on earth. When I look into his face and see the light reflected in the eyes that so closely resemble those of my children, I am reminded of a wonderful saying from the Hasidic Rabbi, the Ba'al Shem Tov:

"From every human being there rises a light that reaches straight to heaven. And when two souls that are destined to be together find each other, their streams of light flow together and a single brighter light goes forth from their united being."

What's in a Name?

$\mathcal{I}$ have trouble with names; not with spelling them, pronouncing them or even remembering them. My problem is simply this: I have trouble choosing names, particularly when it comes to my own.

I discovered this about myself several months before my marriage, during an innocuous conversation about thank you notes with my soon-to-be husband.

"What name do you want to put on the return address?" he asked me innocently enough.

I hesitated for a few moments, feeling like a contestant on a T.V. game show who was about to give the wrong answer.

"I think I'll just keep my own, if that's okay with you," I replied, uncertain if I had just placed myself in double jeopardy.

The problem for me was this: For the first 29 years of my life I had lived with the last name of Hirshberg. I'll admit, the name isn't very sexy or chic, but it was mine and I had grown used to it. During elementary school I got teased because of it (Hirshberg is easily converted into Hershey Bar or Hamburger by an eight year old mind) and in high school, I was taunted because of it. (That's a *Jewish* name, isn't it?) Over the years, I had become both protective and proud of my name. It was a part of me that extended beyond my physical self into the world, but it also did much to define my sense of self.

Yet now that I was joining lives with the man I loved, I knew I had to look at myself in new ways. I wanted to be a team player, really I did, so I gave the name change a few tries. I tried my new identity at work but felt so conflicted that at one point I actually had three different business cards, each one advertising an alternative variation of our combined names. Then there was the message on our answering machine that began with: "You have reached the home of Ray Lederman and Amy Hirshberg, Amy Lederman or Amy Hirshberg Lederman, depending on how I feel today." I knew things had gone too far when MasterCard refused to re-issue my credit card because my hyphenated name didn't fit in the available space.

For approximately the first 15 years of marriage, I changed my name more times than the oil in my car. Then one day I came upon a quote from the Jewish sages that gave me the insight and guidance I needed to finally decide.

"A person is given three names: the one that his parents call him, the one that his fellow man calls him and the one that he acquires by his deeds. But the one he acquires by his deeds is better than all the others."

That bit of Jewish wisdom hit my heart like a heat-seeking missile. I realized that the "deed" which generates the most meaning and satisfaction in my life (as well as plenty of heartache!) is being the parent of my two children. Since the moment I gave birth to my son, and two years later to my daughter, I have felt more deeply connected to life, more aware of its mysteries and more accepting of the unique aspects of each person born on this earth. In my role as a mother, I have been challenged beyond all possible limits, forcing myself to relinquish expectations while opening my heart and mind to multiple perspectives and possibilities. I ask myself daily: Am I doing the best I can for my son; have I overreacted to my daughter? Can I listen better, learn more, or be clearer in my communications with them?

What does all this parental introspection have to do with the name that is now imprinted on my Visa card? Simply, that as the mother of two children with the last name of Lederman, I have come to cherish that name as the one which best depicts my choices and my challenges and has guided and defined much of my growth as an adult.

And so, I embrace that name as the one that best connects me to the deed for which I am most proud, being a part of the family I love.

THE BAR/BAT MITZVAH:
WHAT LIES BENEATH THE PARTY

*W*hen I was growing up there was an advertisement about rye bread that I loved. The theme was simple and it spoke to anyone who enjoyed the thick, chewy stuff. "You don't have to be Jewish to enjoy Levy's real Jewish Rye!" a Native American man on a horse exclaimed while munching on a piece of bread.

I laughed each time I saw it on television and noticed, over the years, that the Native American was replaced by a Chinese chef, an Irish welder and a cute little "church lady." Odd as it seems, the ad had a curious effect on me. As a teenager who wanted more than anything else to be accepted by my non-Jewish friends, it made me feel like I was part of the "in-crowd." If eating Jewish rye bread had become part of mainstream America, then so had I!

Since my rye bread days, I have seen many things Jewish become Americanized. Bagels stores are as plentiful as Starbucks, schools and universities now close for the Jewish High Holidays and words like *mensch* and *chutzpah* are part of the English language.

I have to admit however, that I felt a bit queasy when I read this headline on the front page of the *Wall Street Journal:* "You don't have to be Jewish to want a Bar Mitzvah."

The article was about a teenage girl who, after attending dozens of Bar/Bat Mitzvah parties, asked her parents if she could have one. An unusual request for a Methodist to be sure, but her parents complied by co-hosting a lavish party with two other families that looked like a Bat Mitzvah without the religion. It described this as a national trend; that an increasing number of non-Jewish pre-teens are asking for parties that resemble those of a Bar/Bat Mitzvah.

Maybe I'm losing my sense of the absurd, but it seems like a sad commentary on Jewish tradition when one of the most significant religious rites of passage is reduced to a "me-too!" party that any 13 year old can finagle out of her parents – Jewish or not. And while I hate to admit it, I fear we have no one to blame but ourselves.

In Hebrew the words *Bar Mitzvah* literally mean "son of the commandment." It is an ancient Jewish ritual dating back to the first century C.E., marking the religious and legal coming of age of a Jewish male at 13. The event marks the transition from boyhood to manhood in terms of Jewish communal prayer life, enabling the Bar Mitzvah to be counted as part of the *minyan* (the quorum of ten adults Jewish males necessary for certain prayers) and permitting him to read from the Torah. On an individual level, it establishes the age of legal responsibility and obligation to follow all the commandments.

Originally, the central act of becoming a Bar Mitzvah was the *aliyah,* or being called to bless and read from the Torah. Over time, it became customary for the Bar Mitzvah to deliver a *D'rash,* or commentary, on the portion he had read. In modern times, accomplished Bar and Bat Mitzvah students often lead a significant part of the synagogue service as well.

Because traditionally women did not participate in the performance of public religious rites and communal prayer, there was no parallel ritual for girls until the twentieth century. The first Bat Mitzvah was held in 1922 when the daughter of Mordechia Kaplan, the founder of the Reconstructionist movement, celebrated one. As Jewish adulthood for women is considered to occur at age twelve, a twelve year-old Jewish girl can have a Bat Mitzvah, although traditional synagogues may limit her participation to a discourse on the Torah or Haftorah portion.

Becoming a Bar or Bat Mitzvah requires years of religious training which includes studying Jewish history, holidays, ethics and Hebrew as well as learning to chant from the Torah and Haftorah. It requires attending synagogue services and learning the prayers, blessings and songs. Recently, many synagogues have added a *Tzedakah* (charity) component, emphasizing the Jewish obligation of *tikkun olam* (repairing the world). This enables the child to look beyond his or her world into the larger community with the goal of helping others in need.

But increasingly, American Jews have shifted their priorities from the religious to the social – putting enormous amounts of time, energy and money into creating extravagant parties which offer everything from Broadway revues and Las Vegas casinos to elaborate themes with prizes, clowns, rides and movies. From the many families I have spoken with, I know that a "keeping up with the Goldberg's party" mentality is both stressful and financially taxing. And while I like a good party as much as the next person, placing the emphasis on the party, rather than on the religious significance of the event, diminishes our tradition and sends a skewed message to our family, friends and the non-Jewish world about what a Bar/Bat Mitzvah is all about.

Perhaps it is time for us to step back and reexamine our own relationship with the Bar/Bat Mitzvah experience. For if we focus our energy on the real meaning of the ritual for our children – on the importance of Jewish learning and the need to become personally and spiritually responsible for our actions in this world, we may ourselves feel happier and more fulfilled with the process and the outcome.

THE ART OF PARENTING:
HOLDING ON, LETTING GO

"*R*aise a child and your heart will never be the same," my grandmother told me many years ago while patting her frail, freckled hand over her 98-year-old heart.

Those words came back to me as the plane lifted off the tarmac in Tucson and my own heart plummeted into my stomach. The weeks spent in preparation and the daunting task of packing in no way prepared me for how I would feel when I finally said goodbye to my son. It was a defining moment for us both and we knew it. The shine in his eyes came from his excitement at living away from home for the first time, going to a school that would provide him with wonderful opportunities to grow and make new friends. The glistening in my eyes came from the tears I held back and the painful realization that I was undergoing nothing short of an amputation of the soul.

Raise a child and your heart will never be the same. Not less than a week after Joshua left, those words resurfaced on my morning walk with our dog Wookie (named after the fury creature in the first Star Wars movie). She was wearing a retractable leash, the kind that lets you monitor your dog even when she's a block away. It struck me as I watched Wookie sniff her way through the neighborhood that the art of parenting is much like walking a dog. It requires us to become a retractable leash of love.

As a mother I have struggled with maintaining a balance between holding on and letting go, between giving my children the freedom they need to individuate and maintaining control over their choices to minimize the dangers they will face. Early on when the choices were simple, I held on to the leash loosely with a flexible grip. Peanut butter over macaroni and cheese or naptime versus playtime didn't require me to stretch too much in any one direction. But as decisions became more complex and involved questions about friendship, values, love, God, sex and morality, I felt the taut pull of the leash stretch my parenting skills to the max.

I've spent my fair share of time scanning parenting magazines in the check-out line at the grocery store. I've even consulted experts and counselors on the subject. But when it comes down to it, Jewish wisdom has provided me with some wonderful insights which have helped me in my efforts to become a better parent.

In Judaism, a parent is viewed first and foremost as a teacher. (The Hebrew word for parents, *horeem*, comes from the word *moreh*, or teacher.) We are designated as the teachers of tradition and transmitters of values, responsible for connecting our children to their history, community and faith. The core of this faith is found in the teachings of the Torah which is why, historically, much of Jewish parenting has revolved around giving our children a "good Jewish education." If we are not capable or do not know how to teach them personally, we can ask family members, friends, teachers and rabbis for help. But it is our responsibility to take the lead, to direct and promote the learning that is required to be a good person and a committed Jew.

From the moment our children take their first steps away from us to the day they leave home for good, Judaism expects us to teach them how to live and act so that they will be able to physically, emotionally, financially and spiritually survive in the world. We are required to teach our children Torah to prepare them to live moral and spiritually meaningful lives. We are commanded to teach them how to physically survive in the world, to develop the necessary skills or vocations they will need to become financially self-sufficient. We are entrusted to help them choose a suitable life partner so that they can live emotionally fulfilling lives. Finally, we are required to teach them how to swim in an effort to enable them to feel secure in their physical surroundings.

As any good teacher will tell you, a significant part of teaching is done through modeling the desired behavior or idea you are trying to convey. It is not just what we teach our children but *how* we teach them that is important. Our role as parent is compromised if we fail to model essential Jewish values such as love, compassion, honesty, respect and justice, not only in the way we treat our children but in the way we treat others in our lives as well.

The Jewish view of parent as teacher does a great deal to help us when it is time to let go. For if we have taken the time and effort necessary to teach our children the values and principles that are important to us as human beings and as Jews when they are young, we can take comfort in knowing that we have done our best to prepare them, not only to survive, but to thrive in the world.

LOVING OUR CHILDREN –
SEPARATELY BUT EQUALLY

*M*y son called from college the other night and asked to talk to his sister.

"She's out at a poetry reading," I answered casually. "How are things with you?"

"What do you mean she's OUT?" he exclaimed indignantly. "You let her stay out past 10:00 on a school night?"

I braced myself for the inevitable – the one, consistent complaint that followed me throughout their childhood like a well-trained dog.

"You never let ME do that at her age! That's so unfair!"

I gave him my time-tested answer, the one I always give when my children complain of being treated differently. An answer born from years of parenting which has taught me that diffusing a situation with humor usually works best.

"I let her stay out later than you because I love her more!" I joked. "Besides, her criminal record is shorter than yours."

He laughed for a moment but then his voice turned serious.

"No, mom, I mean it. Why does she get to do so many things differently than I did at her age?"

Whoa! How could I explain to my 19-year-old son that we viewed each of our children with the same loving eyes but recognized from the start that they were unique, special and very different from each other, requiring us to respond differently to them throughout their childhoods? That we made our decisions as parents based on who they were as *individuals* – because of how they acted and related to others, how they felt about themselves, what they loved and hated to do, what made them feel afraid, nervous or tense. Surely it would have been easier to treat them the same, to make uniform decisions that applied across the board. But our parental instincts told us to respond to each child in kind, according to his or her unique temperament, personality and needs as they emerged, even though it wasn't easier or less stressful for us to do so at the time.

From the earliest of times it was understood that a child should be trained according to his mental, emotional and physical abilities. "Educate a child according to his way" the Book of Proverbs teaches us. (22:6) We are cautioned however, to avoid favoring one child over the other because of their unique abilities, blood line or lineage.

Playing favorites with our children can fill a family with jealousy, contempt and hatred and cause rifts that last well beyond the lifetime of the parent.

The Bible is replete with stories of sibling rivalry caused by parental favoritism. Abraham favored Isaac over Ishmael, Rebecca loved Jacob more than Esau, and Jacob loved Joseph more than any of his other 12 children. As Genesis 37:4 tells us: "His brothers saw that their father loved him (Joseph) more than any of his brothers, so they hated him; and they could not speak a friendly word to him."

The rabbis of the Talmud responded to the Joseph story with the following advice: "A man should never single out one of his children for favorable treatment, for because of the two extra coins' worth of silk (which Jacob had woven into Joseph's special coat) Joseph's brothers became jealous of him, and one thing led to another until our ancestors became slaves in Egypt." (Shabbat 10b)

Our children are entitled to feel equally loved and treasured by us, even though this does not always equate into being treated equally by us. To paraphrase the insightful words of Rabbi Irwin Kula: "Loving equally doesn't necessarily mean loving in precisely the same way. To have your children experience that they are loved equally demands that you know how to love them differently because to love them equally means to love them uniquely."

So how do we, as parents, walk the tightrope of responding to our children differently because of their unique needs and personalities while reinforcing in them the knowledge and feeling that they are loved equally by us?

In our home we gave our children different bedtimes, sent them to different summer camps, let them ride the city bus and walk to the mall or a friend's home at different ages; each decision based on their innate needs, abilities, fears and sense of self. For one child, we permitted more after-school activities because she had many diverse interests at the time. For the other, we prohibited nighttime driving for several months longer because directions initially posed a challenge.

When children are little it is hard to explain the reasons and feelings behind our parenting decisions. Yet it is important to take the time to admire their different strengths and assure them that they are loved for who they are.

One way is to create a special time each week to tell them. We created that time every Friday night when we blessed our children. When they were young, we told them out loud what we loved about them and why we loved being their parents. As they got older (and more embarrassed by us), we whispered special blessings in their ears along with the traditional Sabbath blessing for children. It was a time that they counted on, a time we all needed, to celebrate who they were as individuals and remind and reassure them about why and what we loved about them.

In this hectic world where school, work, social, religious and community obligations infringe on precious family time, it becomes even more important to carve out time to assure our children that they are loved, separately but equally, and give them the confidence and support they need to pursue their own unique paths into adulthood.

Cellular Love

$\mathcal{M}$y mother called tonight while I was cooking dinner. Again, for the third time today. I knew who it was because the words "Mom's cell" lit up my own cell phone like a marquee on Times Square. I lay down my cutting knife and shook the pieces of onion and red pepper from my hands. Mom with a cell-phone; boy, have things changed!

There was a time in my life, B.C. (Before Cell phones) when my mother would become anxious, depressed and even mildly hysterical because she couldn't reach me by phone. No matter that I worked full-time and ran a marathon life shuttling kids, groceries and the dog from one end of town to the other. If she called the house and I didn't answer, something had to be wrong.

"Where are you? I've tried a hundred times but you don't answer. Is anybody there?" were the plaintive words I'd find on my answering machine. If my mother got lucky, she'd reach my daughter and tell her to leave me a message, which I'd usually find about a week later written in crayon on the back of the phone bill. "Call gramma. She wants to know if you still live here."

At 78, my mother now lives in a country whose borders are defined by mountains of fear. Its landscape is restricted by age, illness and the loss of much of what and whom she has cherished all her life. The roads she traveled on so easily in her youth have become more treacherous as she loses confidence in her ability to understand and navigate through the world we live in today.

I toss the salad as my mother shares the events of her day: a doctor's appointment for my father who can't see as well as he thinks but she lets him drive anyway, lunch with a friend whose husband has Alzheimer's disease, and an exercise class for osteoporosis even though she's sure the teacher has shrunk two inches since she began taking the class. It doesn't really matter what we talk about. What matters most is the invisible line of connection we create in spite of the time and distance between us.

There are times when she calls and I become irritated by her vast generalizations about people or annoyed that she has told me the same story numerous times. Other times I am too preoccupied or tired to talk, and I simply listen to her while I fold clothes or cook dinner.

Sometimes I wonder if I am being a good daughter. Am I giving her the kind of attention she deserves, listening to her conversation with one ear while the other one is focused on the evening news?

Family relationships, especially those between parents and children, are perhaps the most complex of all relationships. From the beginning of time, they have fascinated the human mind and dominated the human spirit. Nowhere is this more clear than in way the Torah elevates the relationship between parents and children.

The Fifth Commandment tells us what is expected of us as children when it says: "Honor your father and your mother." A passage in Leviticus expands upon this duty by commanding: "Let each of you revere your mother and father." (19:3)

Jewish tradition is clear: the two fundamental obligations that a Jewish child owes his or her parents is to honor and revere them.

According to the Talmud, honoring our parents is expressed through the performance of positive deeds, such as providing them with food, clothing, shelter and assistance. Much like our parents cared for us when we were young and vulnerable, we are expected to do the same for them in their time of need.

Revering our parents is different from honoring them in that it takes the form of restraining from doing certain things, such as not contradicting them in public, taking sides against them or "sitting or standing" in their place. In essence, we do our best as children to avoid causing our parents harm or emotional pain.

These commandments to honor and revere our parents are not without exceptions, however. Judaism does not expect a child to blindly comply with every parental demand if the request is unreasonable or will damage the child's own financial, emotional or spiritual needs. For example, a child can refuse a parent's demand to do something immoral (such as lie) or to violate a Jewish law (such as drive on the Sabbath). Moreover a child is not expected to use his or her own resources (financial as well as psychological) to provide for a parent if the parent has the ability to do so.

I say goodbye to my mother, cell phone falling from my ear like an oversized clip-on earring. I hope that in the days ahead I can give her what she so well deserves – honor, respect, an open heart and willing hand. Whatever the cost or whenever the time, I know she has my number: it's called Cellular Love.

MY GRANDMOTHER'S CANDLESTICKS

I awoke from a sound sleep and bolted upright in the dark room. The digital clock read 6:01 A.M., and the birds had already begun their morning song. I sat very still, my breathing shallow; my heart raced as thought sand feelings overwhelmed me. I knew that she had been here, that she had stood over me while I slept, that she had come to kiss me goodbye. I still felt her warmth on my lips and her undeniable scent permeated the room.

"Grandma," I whispered. "Grandma, where are you?" I wanted so desperately to talk to her, to hold her one more time.

My husband, still asleep, moved closer to me. I touched him lightly on the shoulder. "Ray, wake up honey," I said as I felt the hot tears toll down onto my cheeks. As if in a dream I heard myself say with absolute certainty, "Grandma Edna just died."

Afraid of my intuition, I reached over to turn on the light which is next to my bed. On my nightstand is a picture of Grandma and me, which was taken the last time I was with her. She is holding my daughter Lauren, who is two-and-a half years old at the time. There is a faraway look in Grandma's smiling eyes, betraying the cataracts that plagued her for so many years. Looking at the photograph, I can see our similarities so clearly now that she is gone. Our faces contain the same history; they read like maps of the same territory traveled over different periods of time. Small, pert Russian noses, fair, freckled skin and shining, mischievous eyes. We loved each other without question or hesitation and while the meaning of her world shrunk as the opportunities in mine grew, she never failed to tell me what to do and how to do it.

Born in the small Russian town of Lutsk in 1887, Edna Wolfe left Russia at eighteen months and sailed to America with her two older sisters, her brother and her father. Her own mother was forced to stay behind because she couldn't leave her blind mother alone. When she was finally able to come to America, she traveled with nothing but the clothes on her back. "But she tricked them," Grandma would tell me with a twinkle in her eye. "She hid our *Shabbas* candlesticks in the lining of her winter coat and never took that coat off until she landed in New York."

Those candlesticks were testimony to a way of life; they were the triumph of a broken family fighting to find their way back to one another in a land that promised everything.

Grandma lit those candlesticks every holiday and each Shabbat. She would close her eyes and mumble while swaying back and forth in front of the dancing flames. As a young girl, I thought she knew everything, that the power of the world rested in those small, freckled fingertips that spread the warmth of the candle's light. I saw her as the source of our family tradition, the ultimate word on what we should all do and be.

Some things are easy to remember, like the smell of her kitchen when she was cooking, or the red leather pocketbook she brought me from Mexico for my fifth birthday or the soft, brown leather recliner in her den which smelled like rosewater and my grandpa's aftershave.

Some things I never understood, like her stiffness when Grandpa hugged her or why she never seemed satisfied with her life. I realize now that what she loved best was people. As was common for women of her generation, she had only a fifth-grade education and never felt comfortable in the world of books. Instead, she read people's faces and studied the fine print of their expressions; what they said, what they left out. She defined herself through her children but desperately resented them when they didn't need her anymore.

I asked her one day when I was in high school if she ever wanted to do something, have a career, write a book. She answered without hesitation, "What would I do with all of that? I did what I knew. I cooked, I cleaned, I raised my children. And now they're gone, off with their busy lives, always so busy. I never thought..." Her words trailed off and a distant look crossed her face. In her memories she found not comfort but abandonment and betrayal.

After I graduated college, I would visit her whenever I could. She couldn't understand my need to go, to see the world. In her opinion, I was missing the point. "Raise a family," she told me, "and your heart will never be the same."

It was getting harder for me to share my world of politics, feminism and adventure with her, and I would leave feeling frustrated at how little I was able to communicate. As we both got older however, it became less important for me to make her understand my life because I realized that she still had so much to tell me about hers. She was becoming more afraid of death and needed to talk about her world in order to make sense of it before she died. Why did she feel so discarded, so useless after all the years of being the central force behind her family? Why did not one of her children ask her to come and live with them?

I will never forget the day I visited her in the nursing home just a few months before she died. She had become diminished, not so much by age but the bitter ironies of her life. She seemed happy when I told her about my two children, my husband and the home we had made together. But my law career and the many aspirations I had were of no real interest to her. She held my hand and I stared at the big, brown freckles that covered her skin. She needed so much reassurance now, to know that her life had been meaningful.

I painted her fingernails while we talked and she reminisced about the old days. Of her sisters and the hours they spent laughing together in the kitchen, sharing secrets, when they all lived together in the house on Fair Street. Of my father and what a "prince" he had been but how he never understood her anymore. I sensed in her ramblings that she was in another time and place entirely.

As I got ready to leave, she slowly got up from her chair. She walked toward me and then, changing her mind, headed directly towards the hutch that contained the few remaining items she kept from the old days. She took down the beautiful brass candlesticks that I had loved since I was a little girl.

"My darling girl," she said with watery eyes. "You have always been filled with the love of your Jewishness. May you find joy and meaning in whatever you choose to do with your life. But remember, nothing you do will be more important than your family." She handed me the candlesticks and said, "It is only right that these should belong to you now."

It has been more than a decade since my grandma died. Sometimes all I need is the scent of cinnamon or a jar of Ponds Cold Cream to bring her back to me. But as the years pass, she has become harder and harder to recall. I am certain that is why she gave me her candlesticks. For each time I light the candles, I feel her love for me gently burning in the flames and bestowing upon me the power and inner-strength to create a life of meaning and purpose. And in doing so, I have come to understand the legacy of her life and the meaning of her blessing.

My Grandmother's Candlesticks: Lighting the Way for Others

$\mathcal{I}$ entered the classroom of 32 seventh graders at the worst time imaginable – seventh period on a Friday afternoon, the weekend before Halloween. I knew the deck was stacked against me. I had been warned by the very enthusiastic teacher who asked me to read my short story as part of her unit on ethnic literature, that this class was a "rowdy" group.

I came prepared with two grocery bags, one filled with boxes of donuts and soda and the other with my copy of *Chicken Soup for the Jewish Soul* and my grandmother's candlesticks. I knew one thing for certain; even if the students didn't understand my story, they would appreciate the Jewish tradition that learning should be a sweet experience. Munching on donuts while listening to me read would capture their stomachs, if not their hearts.

I scanned the overcrowded classroom; typical adolescents sporting pimples, nose rings, hair gel and Attitude. When the teacher introduced me as the local Tucson author who wrote a short story called "Grandmother's Candlesticks," eyes rolled, chairs tilted back and notebooks opened in preparation for some serious doodling.

I would have given anything for my grandmother to be able to see what transpired in the classroom that day. For in the period of less than an hour, a multi-cultural group of boisterous teens came together in a rare moment of understanding, compassion and kinship.

How did the story about a pair of brass candlesticks secretly brought over from Russia in the lining of a coat capture the minds and hearts of children who had never heard of a pogrom or of the Jewish Sabbath? Why did the image of my aging grandmother struggling to remain central in the lives of her children touch their imaginations and their souls? And who would have imagined that as I read about my grandmother handing me the candlesticks with her blessing before she died, students would break down sobbing, remembering their own grandmothers, aunts, uncles and parents who had died too soon, leaving them with too little?

When I finished reading, I passed the heavy brass candlesticks, covered in years of wax, up and down the rows of students. It was as if they felt the weight of tradition in their hands as they gently handed the candlesticks to one another. I asked if anyone wanted to share their feelings or ask me questions about what I wrote.

At first no one spoke. A pale-looking girl stood and walked to the front of the room, sniffling and wiping her nose with the back of her sleeve. She asked if she could read a poem she had written for her father who had died in the hospital less than three months before. She had been carrying it around with her since he died, but had never read it to anyone. In a child's whisper, she spoke directly to her father in couplet form, without hesitation or fear. As she walked back to her seat, friends crowded around her hugging her small frame, handing her a Kleenex, offering her support.

Then a tough-looking young man who had scribbled throughout my reading stood up and told his story. He didn't have a grandmother or a grandfather, he said, or even a mother. They had all been killed by a drunk driver when he was four. He wished he had something like the brass candlesticks, something they had shared together with old wax or fingerprints on it, because it was like having a piece of them with you forever.

As child after child told of a "tia," "abuela" or "nana" with whom they had lived, loved and lost, the classroom became a sanctuary for years of unspoken grief. The bell rang but no one wanted to leave.

I gathered my things, hugged a few of the students and said goodbye. I had almost reached my car when I heard someone call my name.

Turning towards the voice, I stared into the face of Celeste, one of the students in the class who hadn't said a word.

"Would you please talk to my father?" she implored. "I really want to go to Phoenix – to the cemetery to see my grandpa – he died a while ago – I can't get there by myself – I have to go but he won't take me."

Her words came out like choked staccato notes; short, sharp and pointed.

"Well, honey, I could call him if you want but..."

"You don't have to," she interrupted, "he's sitting right over there in that pick-up truck."

I slowly turned my head and saw a very big truck across the parking lot. I walked towards it and awkwardly looked into the face of a man I had never met. Swallowing my discomfort, I told him how much it would mean to his daughter if she could visit her grandfather's grave; to have the chance to tell him what was on her mind and in her heart.

He grunted, said he'd think about it, and revved the engine which was my signal that the conversation had ended. I felt badly, thinking that I hadn't helped the situation much and that Celeste would never have the closure she so desperately needed with her grandfather.

Weeks later I received a letter on notebook paper from Celeste. Tears filled my eyes when I read her words. Her father had taken her to Phoenix to visit her grandfather. She was lucky, she said, because now she could visit him whenever they went there. She had written me the letter so that I would have something permanent to keep by which to remember her. Not as nice as those candlesticks, she wrote, but something special just the same.

$\mathcal{H}$OLIDAYS

ROSH HASHANAH: IT'S NEVER TOO LATE TO GET IT RIGHT!

$\mathcal{H}$ow many times have you been on a car trip with a small child and a squeaky, somewhat irritable voice emerges from the back seat only to ask: "Are we *there* yet?"

From the earliest of ages, we tend to view life not so much in terms of where we are at any given moment, but where we want to be or think we should be. This point hit home on a trip my family made one August to San Diego. Armed with a cache of books, game boys, headphones and cds, they entered the car like soldiers settling in for a siege. Silly me, I actually thought we'd use the road time to talk. But the car ride was just a means to an end; it had to be endured in order to get to the beaches and boogie boards they were ultimately after.

I think a lot about that trip during the closing days of August. Not because it is unbearably hot in Tucson and the beaches of San Diego would be a welcome respite. But because during the Jewish month of Elul, the 30 days preceding Rosh HaShanah, we are challenged as Jews to think about where we are right now, where we have been in the past year and where we want to go in the coming year

– as individuals, as a family, as a community and as members of the world. The Jewish tradition teaches that Rosh HaShanah marks the birth of the world and the creation of humankind. But rather than being a holiday of Jewish history, it is really a holiday of personal history. Rosh HaShanah presents us with the opportunity every year of our lives to engage in meaningful questioning and introspection that can become the catalyst for personal renewal. We link ourselves to the first Creation because we are "reborn" through the efforts we take to renew ourselves spiritually in positive ways. Rosh HaShanah tells us in no uncertain terms that for Jews, it's never too late to get it right.

Rosh HaShanah is like an annual performance review of the soul. In most jobs, performance is evaluated regularly to determine if we are eligible for a raise. During the ten days between Rosh HaShanah and Yom Kippur, we are asked to evaluate ourselves to see if we have met our spiritual goals, to see if we are eligible for a "spiritual raise." We ask ourselves: What am I doing with my life? Am I accomplishing what I set out to do? Where have I failed, where have I succeeded? What do I want to change in the coming year? Can I be better person, a more compassionate friend, a more caring daughter, a more attentive father, a more supportive spouse? This type of hard questioning is called a *heshbone nefesh,* an accounting of the soul.

But here comes the tricky question: Is there anything we can actually do to guarantee becoming a better person? Can we take steps now to get the spiritual raise we seek in the coming year?

An answer I've found that reflects the spirit of the holiday as well as the essence of Judaism itself is this: We can add a *mitzvah* (Hebrew for commandment) every year to our life.

Judaism doesn't expect us to do everything at once but encourages us to question, seek and grow throughout our lives. We can raise ourselves one step at a time if we commit to doing one of the 613 commandments every Rosh HaShanah. They cover the broadest spectrum imaginable – from ritual observance to family and community relationships to business dealings – and you don't have to be "religious" or even particularly knowledgeable to begin.

Just look around you – in your home, at your work place or in your relationships – to determine what it is that you want to improve upon in the coming year. Do you want to help others more? Would you like to learn Hebrew? Do you wish you didn't gossip so much? Is there someone who is ill that you should visit?

If you have trouble choosing what mitzvah you want to do, consult a rabbi, teacher or respected friend or buy a good book on basic Judaism and begin to explore your options. Don't let lack of knowledge or the feeling that you won't do it right get in your way!

My family has been adding a *mitzvah* a year since our children were little. One year we decided to light candles and make Shabbat every Friday night. Another year we took the plunge and kashered our home. Some commitments took more time and effort but every decision we made has added to the richness of our Jewish experience and brought us closer as a family. And with each new year we hope to improve ourselves – one *mitzvah* at a time.

CHANUKAH: A CELEBRATION
OF JEWISH SPIRIT

We could have been in Poland or Russia more than a hundred years ago, such were the images and sounds surrounding us. But it was 1997 and we were in Jerusalem. A brisk wind blew across our faces as we walked though the crowded streets of Mea Shearim, an ultra-orthodox neighborhood overflowing with people, noise and religious fervor. Israeli soldiers guarded the entrance to the street, protecting those who lived there.

We arrived at dusk, just in time to watch the amazing transition from earthly darkness to spiritual light. Fathers, mothers, grandparents, uncles and rows of children stood in full view of kitchen and dining room windows, each person lighting candles on their own *Hanukkiah* (menorah) as is the custom in Ashkenazi families. The street lit up like the Milky Way, hundreds of candles sparkling overhead. My family marveled at the sight.

"It's like the street is one big birthday cake!" my ten year old daughter squealed with delight. Her remark hit me as deeply insightful: Chanukah in its truest sense is a celebration of the re-birth of Jewish spirituality and self-actualization.

The story of Chanukah I learned as a child is well known and often cited as the archetypal example of Jewish resistance against assimilation. In 168 B.C.E. the Syrian King Antiochus desecrated the Temple in Jerusalem with pagan gods and impure animals and waged a campaign to obliterate Jewish rituals like circumcision and Shabbat. Mattathias the High Priest, father of Judah the Maccabee, refused to succumb to pagan idol worship and led his five sons and a band of ragtag Jewish farmers into the caves of the Judean desert with the rallying cry of "Whoever is for God, follow me!"

For three years this small band of Jews fought in fierce guerilla warfare against the well-equipped, well-trained Syrian army. On the 25th of Kislev, the Maccabees succeeded in restoring the sanctity of the Holy Temple and rededicated it to God. We learn from the letters on the dreidel that "A Great Miracle Happened There" when a miniscule amount of ritual oil lasted for eight days until more could be found to keep the Temple's sacred Menorah lit.

But there is a story within this story which is not as well known. For while Chanukah is the only important festival in the Jewish calendar not mentioned anywhere in the Hebrew Bible, it is also one of the few festivals for which definitive historical records exist.

Within 25 years of the rededication of the Holy Temple, the First Book of Maccabees was written which chronicled the events from eyewitness accounts and historical records of the Hellenistic period. The book depicts the Maccabees' accomplishments in religious and nationalistic terms. They fought for God so that they could carry out His plan for a just world. It is a story of might and spirit, of the rebirth of Jewish ritual and observance through the physical efforts of the Jewish people.

But here's where an interesting bit of historical revisionism occurs. Approximately 400 years later when the Talmudic rabbis described the holiday of Chanukah, they never mentioned the valiant struggle or even the word Maccabee. Rather, they emphasized God's saving spirit and highlighted the story about the single cruse of oil which miraculously burned for eight days. Why?

The rabbis were no dummies; their interpretation was diplomatic and politically savvy. By the time they wrote the Talmud, the Hasmonean dynasty (direct descendants of the Maccabees) had been highly discredited as a group of corrupt Jewish rulers who tried to usurp the Davidic line of kingship. The rabbis did not want to associate the holiday with the military victory that led to the rise of this degenerate dynasty. Nor did they want to raise a red flag of rebelliousness in the face of the Roman Empire under which they lived by emphasizing the successful Jewish overthrow of oppressive foreign rule. And so, in their wisdom, they shifted the significance of Chanukah from the physical to the spiritual, awakening the spirit of the Jewish people with the miracle of the rekindling of the lights.

Inasmuch as rabbinic tradition minimized the physical prowess of the Maccabees, modern Zionism and the state of Israel, which identified with the Maccabees, has often been antagonistic towards rabbinic tradition. Yet this need not be the case. The dual interpretations of Chanukah represent two essential approaches to the survival of Judaism and the Jewish people – the physical and the spiritual.

Like the Israeli soldiers who faithfully protect the religious Jews in Mea Shearim, Chanukah reminds us of the importance of this piece of Jewish wisdom: "Pray as if everything depends upon God but act as if everything depends upon you."

PURIM AND THE UNTOLD TALE OF ABUSE

*T*he Book of Esther, contained in the *Ketuvim* (or Writings) section of the Bible, is read on the holiday of Purim. It tells the story of a young Jewish girl named Esther and her Uncle Mordechia, who together foil a plot by Haman, the wicked advisor to King Ahashveros, to kill all the Persian Jews. The story opens with the King's drunken request that his wife, Queen Vashti, appear before him "adorned with the royal crown, to show off to the people and the officials her beauty, for she was beautiful of appearance." (Book of Esther 1:10) The text never directly states what it is that the King wanted Vashti to do. Jewish tradition suggests that she was expected to dance naked before the dinner guests; modern scholarship posits that perhaps she was to participate in an after-dinner orgy as if she were a concubine rather than a queen. From either point of view, it is plausible to surmise that Vashti was in an abusive relationship.

In a bold move, Vashti refuses to come and the King, infuriated by her refusal, asks his advisors what to do. They interpret Vashti's assertiveness as a direct assault not only on the King but on all the husbands in the Empire. For this, she is publicly banned from the King's sight forever and her royal estate is confiscated with the intent that it be conferred upon another woman better than she. The decree is spread throughout the kingdom so that all the wives understand the dire consequences of disobeying their husbands.

Traditionally, it is Esther and Mordechia who are portrayed as the heroes of the Purim story because they succeed in foiling Haman's plan of Jewish genocide. We feel heartened when we read about Esther's bravery in approaching the King unsummoned (an act punishable by death) in order to expose herself as a Jewess and undermine Haman's plan to kill the Jewish people. We feel inspired when we learn that Mordechai refused to bow down to

Haman and helped Esther to understand that her mission as Queen was to save the Jews. We are raucous in synagogue when we boo and shake our noisy greggers at the mention of the wicked name of Haman. Yet we don't think much about the deposed Queen Vashti, even though her removal as Queen prepared the way for Esther to take her place.

I have always viewed Vashti as a heroine in her own right. Although not central to the story, Vashti provides a model of empowerment for women in abusive situations who are afraid to speak out or take action. And while Vashti herself was not a Jew; it is clear from national and international studies conducted by Hadassah and Jewish Women International that relationship abuse does occur in Jewish families.

Studies estimate that 15 to 20 percent of Jewish women are in abusive relationships, a rate comparable to that of non-Jewish women. Jewish women are known to stay longer with abusive men than non-Jewish women by an average of five to seven years. And while there are no real denominational differences (i.e., the rate of violence is the same among Orthodox, Conservative and Reform Jews), observant Jewish women often feel that by admitting abuse, they also admit to their failure to promote the Jewish value of *shalom bayit* (peace in the home) and thus are more reluctant to do so.

Because the prevailing assumption is that domestic abuse does not occur in Jewish families, many Jewish women are reluctant to seek help. They are afraid of the reactions they might get from family members and friends – reactions of disbelief, disgust and disappointment.

Unlike Vashti, who alone confronted her husband's abuse, Jews today have many resources to turn to for help. There are international, national and local organizations that provide help and information about abusive relationships. These resources encourage victims of abuse to speak out and teach communities to respond in ways that will help those in need find emotional and physical safety, healing and justice.

The Jewish National Resource on Domestic Violence, Shalom Task Force, has a hotline which provides information on rabbinic, legal and psychological services for anyone in the Jewish community. (1-888-883-2323) The Association of Jewish Family and Children Services (AJFCA) is the umbrella organization for Jewish social and human services organizations throughout the US and Canada, and can help locate a place in your Jewish community where counseling, emergency assistance and crisis intervention is available (ajfca@ajfca.org).

Most Jewish communities have organizations that provide a continuum of services that address the issues of domestic abuse. Purim reminds and encourages all of us to take responsibility to help victims of domestic violence wherever they are.

Passover: Creating a Seder Your Family Will Love!

$\mathcal{I}$t all started almost a decade ago when my husband and I decided that we wanted to create a more personal Passover experience for our family and friends. My own childhood memories were filled with images of my father hunting through our basement for the Maxwell House Haggadahs and my grandmother wrinkling her nose at the gefilte fish my mother served from the jar. Although we weren't what you'd call a religious family, Passover was the one holiday we celebrated every year in our home.

My husband and I wanted to get away from the rote experience of reading the Haggadah and wondered if we could create a Seder experience that would have more meaning for us as a family and as Jews in the 21st century. We took our lead from a line in the Haggadah that states "in every generation we should regard ourselves as though we personally left Egypt." A challenging idea to be sure, but one we hoped we could bring into being with some creative thinking.

We came upon the idea of holding our Seder in a totally different setting. We transformed our back porch into a huge Egyptian tent by hanging sheets from the rafters which were painted with brightly-colored pyramids, camels and sphinxes. Our children hung their Passover art dating back to pre-school days throughout the tent. We spread blankets on the floor and put pillows around the sides to sit or lean back on in accordance with the tradition that we should be relaxed during the Seder. The ceiling was covered with tiny sparkling lights which looked like stars as the evening sun set and the tent became darker. In the corner, encircled by lights, was a beautiful picture of Jerusalem with the words "Next Year in Jerusalem."

As the more than 30 guests arrived, we asked them to remove their shoes like the Hebrew slaves who often worked without them. Each family sat together, near a "Seder Station" – a tray with a Seder plate, matzah, wine, and bowls of parsley, charoset, maror and salt water. Because we had so many children at our Seder, we passed trays of fruit and vegetables during the Seder to ward off hunger and whining. As the years progressed, we asked our friends to contribute more to the Seder itself than just food; to lead a discussion, share a story or offer a reading or poem.

We asked our children to help us create living plagues, which they did with joy. They taped plastic bugs under the cups for "lice", put white styrofoam packing material on our ceiling fan which whirled through the air as "hail" and turned water into "blood." Stomachs were covered with fake boils and sunglasses were passed out to experience the darkness. One year, my son used his fog machine to create an eerie rendition of the killing of the first born and my daughter and her best friend wrote a Passover Rap that rivaled Motown! As our family grew into this experience, we modified, added, and removed things that no longer fit our ages and stages to keep it fresh and meaningful.

When it came time for the festive meal, we exited the tent and followed signs through the sandy desert (our sandbox) to the Promised Land of our backyard where tables were decorated in a Jerusalem motif of blue and gold. We ate under the stars and finished the Seder by singing so loud that one year we even competed with our neighbors in a round of "Dayenus!"

While Passover in a tent is not for everyone, for those of you looking for ways to create more meaningful, lively Seder experiences, here are a few ideas that can help you create one for your family.

Be prepared – Study the Passover text beforehand and

familiarize yourself with the actual story and order of the
Seder so that you can blend your own innovative ideas,
questions and theatrics with Jewish tradition to create a
Seder experience most suitable for your family.

Choose a Haggadah that you like – We used various
Haggadot throughout the years but one of our favorites was
Noam Zion's *A Different Night: A Family Participation
Haggadah*. A quick search online will lead you to wonderful
ideas and books including the newest on the subject enti-
tled *Creating Lively Passover Seders, A Sourcebook of Engaging
Tales, Texts and Activities* (Jewish Lights Publishing).

Be inclusive – Try to engage adults and children at your
Seder by giving them jobs such as thinking up a plague,
acting out a part of the Seder or leading a discussion. The
more your guests feels connected to the Seder itself, the
more meaning it will have for them.

Ask questions – The Hagaddah invites questions and so
should you! Try asking your guests beforehand to think of
a Passover question they would like answered at the Seder
or lead a discussion by asking your guests what "plagues"
them most in their own lives. By encouraging questions
you will encourage your guests to personally explore what
the Seder means to them.

Buy time and use props – Everyone knows that the Seder
is a long night, especially the children. The more you do to
keep the children at your Seder involved, like using toy
plagues and offering snacks during the Seder, the better
your chances for enjoying the time together as you tell the
Passover story.

Celebrate the joy! – Most importantly, Passover is a time
to share the joy of being together as a family in a land
where we are free to practice Judaism openly and rejoice in
the feeling of rebirth and renewal which is the message of
Passover. Whatever you do and however you do it, have fun!

SHAVUOT: A NIGHT OF STUDY, A LIFETIME OF COMMITMENT

The first time I fully experienced the glorious holiday of Shavuot was a balmy June night in Jerusalem. Determined to celebrate the ancient ritual of *tikkun liel Shavuot* (staying up all night to study Torah and other sacred Jewish texts), my husband and I made the necessary childcare arrangements and drank cups of coffee with dinner in preparation for what we imagined would be a spiritual marathon. I'll admit I was nervous, both about the sitter we hired (who knew less English than we knew Hebrew) and about the possibility that I might not be able to make it through the night without falling asleep over the texts.

The crowd of people outside the Pardes Institute where we chose to study buzzed with anticipation as we waited for the doors to open. The old timers came prepared with canteens of soda, thermoses of hot coffee and pillows to sit on. I brought a pen and some no-doze, just in case.

We studied from the book of Exodus with great scholars like Dr. Aviva Zornberg and Rabbi Danny Landis. We discussed the Revelation at Mt. Sinai, what it must have been like then and what it means to receive the Torah in our own day. We struggled with the texts, interpreting difficult passages while plates of cookies and fruit were passed around the room. The hours flew by but instead of feeling tired, I was exhilarated by the many views that were shared. The fact that we all didn't necessarily agree with one another was far less important than the act of grappling with the texts together, as Jews have done for thousands of years.

About an hour before sunrise, we ended our study session and headed through the darkened streets towards the Old City. An ethereal dance of silhouettes moved all around us as thousands of people, many dressed in traditional Chasidic black coats and hats, walked with the same goal in mind – to arrive at the Western Wall by sunrise in time to say the morning prayer service.

Originally Shavuot was celebrated as a spring harvest festival, the time when Jews would make a pilgrimage to the Temple in Jerusalem to offer their first fruits. When sacrifices could no longer be offered because of the destruction of the Second Temple in 70 C.E., the Talmudic rabbis imbued the holiday with spiritual significance by designating it as the day the Israelites received the Torah at Mt. Sinai. They were able to do this because the Torah does not mention any specific date for this momentous event.

In Exodus 19:1 it says that the Israelites arrived at Mt. Sinai "on this day" (*bayom hazeh* in Hebrew). The rabbis interpreted "on this day" to mean that the giving and receiving of the Torah is a perpetual and continuing process which occurs for each person in every generation. The actual date therefore transcends all limitations of time and place. Through the process of interpreting time markers in Exodus and linking various Biblical verses however, the rabbis were able to affix the date of the giving of the Torah as the 6th of Sivan, 50 days after the first counting of the Omer which begins on the second day of Passover. The fiftieth day coincides with Shavuot.

The importance of linking Passover with Shavuot is central to the Jewish idea of redemption. The Exodus from Egypt unified the Israelites as a physical nation by uniting them as a people through their liberation from generations of slavery. They achieved freedom together under the leadership of Moses, who spoke to them of the saving power, might and greatness of God. But for what were they freed?

The answer came three months later at the foot of Mt. Sinai when the Hebrew people became a spiritual nation, unified in the covenant they entered into with the God that brought them out of Egypt "with a strong hand

and an outstretched arm." They were freed for a special purpose and mission – to love God, follow the laws of the Torah and become a holy nation. Redemption and Revelation, physical and spiritual liberation, are intimately linked through Jewish history.

The sun was rising as we reached the *Kotel,* its golden rays spread over the massive stones worn by age and the millions of hands that have clung to it for strength, wisdom and faith. A sea of bodies swayed back and forth and the hum of Hebrew prayers was almost deafening. We stood together in the early morning light – a tapestry of Israeli, American, Canadian, European, South African and Oriental Jews, calling out to history and God in different voices but calling out together, as the Jewish nation did at Sinai several thousand years ago.

As we headed home for breakfast, I understood the significance of staying up all night to study the Torah. The commitment to study reaffirms our relationship to the text, to the Jewish people and to God. Just as we celebrate marriage annually with an anniversary, Shavuot is the time to celebrate the marriage between God and the Jewish people and honor all that has occurred throughout our history to keep Judaism alive and well.

Tisha B'Av: The Jewish
Response to Tragedy

J never really heard of Tisha B'Av when I was growing up. Although my family celebrated major Jewish holidays like Rosh HaShanah and Passover, I was totally unfamiliar with the less-known holidays of Shmini Atzeret, Tisha b'Av and Lag B'Omer.

It wasn't until my junior year in college at Hebrew University in Jerusalem that I learned about Tisha B'Av, a holiday that was jokingly called Tushie-Bottom by my irreverent friends. Paradoxically, our lightheartedness failed to appreciate that Tisha B'Av (the ninth day of the Hebrew month of Av) is the saddest day of the Jewish calendar year – the day which officially commemorates national Jewish mourning.

Tisha B'Av is the anniversary of the destruction of the First Temple in Jerusalem in 586 B.C.E. and the destruction of the Second Temple in 70 C.E. by the Romans. With an uncanny sense of historic irony, it is also the date of some of the worst disasters and expulsions that occurred in Jewish history.

In 1190, Tisha B'Av marked the day that the Jews of York, England were slaughtered; it was also the day Jews were expelled from England one hundred years later. It commemorated the imprisonment of the Jews in France in 1305 and marked the expulsion of the Jews from Spain in 1492 by King Ferdinand and Queen Isabella. Italy ghettoized its Florence Jews on Tisha B'Av in 1571 and Austria forced its Jews out of Vienna in 1670.

The devastating pattern of deportation and death continued into the modern age beginning with Russia's mobilization towards World War I on the ninth of Av, which led to the expulsion of all Jews from the border provinces a year later. The Nazis took pleasure in organizing murderous actions against the Jewish community on Tisha B'Av, such as commencing the deportations from the Warsaw Ghetto to the death camps at Treblinka. The Jewish religious responses to these events were identical to those that are followed when a family member dies. Extensive mourning rituals were developed by the Talmudic rabbis to help the community deal with the profound grief they would continue to experience from the loss of the holy Temple. Today, more than 2,500 years after the destruction of the First Temple, we continue to engage in traditional mourning practices such as fasting, restricting our physical comfort by not bathing, wearing leather shoes, makeup or perfume, and refraining from sexual relations. The public reading of Lamentations occurs in synagogues while congregants often sit on the floor or low stools in the traditional style of mourners.

In some ways, Tisha B'Av is the holiday that reminds us that the Jewish way of life – its traditions, practices, culture and land – have been targeted for extinction since the beginning of Jewish time. History bears witness to a multiplicity of efforts to eradicate the heart and soul of the Jewish people by deporting them from the land of Israel, destroying their religious centers of worship and physically isolating or removing them from community life.

But what history has repeatedly failed to recognize is this singular amazing fact: Each time Jewish survival is threatened, the Jewish response that emerges is one of hope and defiance. Tragedy has always been a catalyst for Jewish national, religious and personal introspection. Jewish leaders, from Ezra the prophet to Theodor Herzl, have responded to Jewish tragedies by using them as an opportunity to build upon the Jewish belief that redemption is possible for every Jew and for the Jewish nation as a whole.

Since the creation of the first Jewish Community Center (the *Bet Knesset*) in Babylon to the creation of the state of Israel, Jews have responded to historic crises with two words: faith and community. Faith, that if we live according to the commandments, we will be restored to the land of Israel and knowledge that we must live, work, study and bond together as a community to guarantee Jewish survival.

Just as Rosh HaShanah provides us with the opportunity each year to engage in meaningful questioning and soulful introspection, Tisha B'Av serves as a time to appreciate what has kept Jews and Judaism alive throughout history: abiding faith and commitment to preserving Jewish community.

THE JEWISH SABBATH: TIME TO PUT MY OCTOPUS TO BED

J have a problem sleeping. To be more precise, I have a problem sleeping past 6:00 in the morning. No matter that it's the weekend or I've stayed up late the night before; when the sun rises, so do I.

This is not something I'm proud of – like a rigorous training schedule I endure in order to run a marathon someday. It is simply a childhood habit that I have been unable to break.

It all started in the spring of my tenth year when my father decided I was officially old enough to become a "full working member" of our family. For him this meant that I was the primary beneficiary of a 6:00 a.m. wake up call that could be heard in the next county. For me it meant the end of any hope of watching cartoons and a list of chores that had to be done before noon.

The net result of this early morning ritual was twofold. First, it turned me into a morning person. You know the type: disgustingly cheerful and perky after having accomplished half a day's work before most people have even brushed their teeth. Second, it taught me Dad's Number One Life Lesson: To live is to work. (Not to be confused with Mom's Number One Life Lesson: To live is to worry.)

Don't get me wrong. Getting up early definitely had its advantages – like being the first one in our family to claim the prize in the Frosted Flakes box or having grown-up conversations with my Dad about things like mortgages and snow blowers. Yet the afterglow of these small victories did not outweigh the long-term negative effect of equating rest with something I've earned only after all of my chores are done.

Over the years the fallacy of this way of thinking has become painfully clear for the simple reason that getting all of my chores done is as probable as putting an octopus to bed. As soon as I have finished wrestling three arms into submission, two more emerge demanding my attention. Regardless of how many meals I cook, how much mail I open or how many hours I spend at the computer, there is always another phone call to return or one more column to write – all with my name on it!

I'm not alone in this struggle; I watch as my friends and co-workers juggle family, career and community life with barely enough time to breathe. On the never-ending treadmill of life's demands, we can't seem to find the "off" button.

From the beginning of time, Jews have been commanded to differentiate between work and rest, between doing and being. We are taught that God created the world in six days and blessed the seventh day as holy because He rested from all that He had created. *Shabbat* (the Hebrew word for Sabbath) is a weekly holiday which teaches us what it means to stop, if only for a while.

The Jewish Sabbath begins on Friday night at sundown and lasts until Saturday evening. It has been called "a sanctuary in time," a holy framework that permits us to stop and reflect on how rich our lives can be when we relinquish control over the things we dominate during the week. It is meant to free us from the pressures and burdens of work, carpool and errands and enable us to renew ourselves through weekly relaxation, spiritual rest and renewal.

Shabbat is an invitation to enjoy time with family and friends, to share a good meal, to pray with our community, to finally finish the last chapter of the book we put down weeks ago for lack of time. It establishes a specific time each week during which we are entitled, even required, to pause and contemplate rather than to do and create.

Our sages taught that "More than Israel has kept the Shabbat, Shabbat has kept Israel." The meaning of this becomes clear when I see how I become a better mother, a more attentive wife, a more caring daughter, and ultimately a more engaged Jew, when I put the weekly demands of my work away in order just "to be."

Shabbat gives me an opportunity to put my octopus to bed. It helps me focus on what is most important in my life and teaches me the discipline of *not doing*. And while I know that there will still be clothes to wash and bills to pay when Shabbat is over, I always feel better for having let go, if only for a while.

ROSH HODESH – A TIME OF RENEWAL

On a warm August evening in 1997, I attended my first
Rosh Hodesh group in a tiny apartment in Jerusalem to
celebrate the cycle of the new moon. I had no idea at the
time what a Rosh Hodesh group actually did but a dear
friend convinced me to go along with her, so I did.

I entered the candle-lit apartment filled with women I
did not know and immediately felt at home. Aromas of my
childhood permeated the room: the smell of olive oil, garlic
and lemon beckoned me to peek into the tiny kitchen
where three women worked shoulder-to-shoulder preparing
food. Platters of stuffed grape leaves, plates of hummus and
eggplant and bowls of dried fruit and nuts lined the counter
top. My stomach confirmed what my mind already knew: I
had come to the right place.

We gathered together in a circle and found seats
wherever there was room. Some of us sat on the couch,
others on the floor or the windowsill overlooking the Old
City of Jerusalem. We were a mixture of faces, races and
generations. To my right sat a small Moroccan woman with
a nose ring and to my left sat a silver-haired woman with a
British accent. Sunburned and freckled, I sat in the middle
wearing bib overalls and a University of Arizona T-shirt.

We began the evening with the ancient Jewish ritual of
acknowledging who we were through the lineage of our
mothers. We introduced ourselves not as Amy or Elaine but
as Amy, daughter of Elise, daughter of Jeanette, daughter of
Sol. And then, as if pulled in by the power of the moon
itself, we began telling our stories.

Woman by woman, country by country, generation by
generation, we peeled away the layers of our defenses to
uncover the history of our lives. Long after the last candle
had burned out, we huddled together talking, listening,
laughing and crying. No one wanted to leave the sanctity of

that room; no one wanted to break the sacred ties we had created between us.

Since that night I have learned that Rosh Hodesh is not a new age concept but a very ancient one. In the First Temple period, before the Jewish lunar calendar was fixed, *Rosh Hodesh* (Hebrew for head of the month) was a holiday of great significance because the dates for all other holidays were based on the sighting of the new moon. The new moon's appearance was communicated to Jewish communities throughout Israel and the Diaspora by setting fires on the hilltops of Jerusalem, starting a chain reaction so that each community lit its own fire to alert its neighbors. Upon its sighting, sacrifices were offered, incense was burned, special prayers were chanted, festive meals were eaten and the shofar was blown.

Traditions pertaining to Rosh Hodesh have changed since the days of sacrifices and feasts. The holiday is observed eleven times each year (we skip it during the month of Tishre, because Rosh HaShanah celebrates the new year as well as the new month) and is celebrated by reciting special blessings and prayers in synagogue.

Rosh Hodesh has traditionally been identified as sacred for the women of Israel. According to tradition, the holiday was given to the women because they refused to surrender their jewelry for the making of the Golden Calf. As a result of their righteousness, they were not required to work on Rosh Hodesh, ate festive meals and lit candles.

From the 16th to the early 20th century, women of Eastern Europe wrote special, personal Rosh Hodesh prayers on the sighting of the new moon called *tekhines,* expressing their innermost thoughts, feelings and hopes. The emergence of the feminist movement in the late 1960's inspired Jewish women to create new venues to discuss and explore their relationship to Jewish ritual, prayer, spirituality and community. Rosh Hodesh groups blossomed in apartments and dorm rooms across the country as a natural vehicle to bring Jewish women together to engage in meaningful Jewish conversation.

Over the past three decades, Rosh Hodesh groups have become a staple in the Jewish women's spiritual diet, providing a safe place to develop new rituals, discuss texts, develop prayer groups and provide support and encouragement for Jewish women worldwide.

Rosh Hodesh groups exist in most towns and cities, either through local synagogues, Hadassah or the Jewish Federation. In addition, books like *Miriam's Well, Rituals for Jewish Women Around the Year* by Penina Adelman and *Moonbeams, A Hadassah Rosh Hodesh Guide* by Leora Tanenbaum are valuable resources if you want to start a group of your own.

Rosh Hodesh is a beautiful holiday which provides Jews with the monthly opportunity to recognize the power of renewal and realize that we all have the chance to begin again.

THE EVERYDAY ORDINARY

A JEWISH VIEW OF MONEY

My husband Ray is a better person than I. He picks up his towels in the hotel bathroom while I surreptitiously take extra soap and shampoo from the cleaning cart in the hall. He gives the waiter a twenty percent tip even when the service is lousy, resulting in an appreciative smile and better service next time. I nitpick about the absence of mushrooms in my soup which earns me the disdain of my family and a free drink.

When it comes to money, he is truly a mensch. I learned this about him during the first year of marriage. We were living on a budget that required more monitoring than the national debt as we struggled to pay off medical and law school bills and establish a home of our own. One day I opened our mail and discovered that our savings account had been credited with ten thousand dollars. My heart soared as I thought of how great it would be to be free of debt but when I shared the good news with Ray, his response was immediate and clear. The money was not ours, never was and never would be. We had no right to it and our only obligation was to contact the bank immediately so they could correct the error. I swallowed hard and thanked God that this man would guide me into my old age (and keep me out of trouble!).

Five years later when Ray was in private practice, he received a substantial check from an insurance company as payment for a patient he thought would never be able to cover the cost of treatment. He had given up any expectation of ever being paid and when he got the check, he told me something I will never forget. "This money isn't mine. I gave up any hope of collecting it when I began treating him. It belongs back in the community, helping other people."

I smiled and looked at our worn couch, which would remain with us for yet another year.

What I have realized over the years is that my husband's view of money is very Jewish. Long before we began our life together, and without any tutoring or course in Jewish studies, he knew exactly how to treat the money he acquired.

The Talmud teaches that a righteous person understands that we do not really own the money we have. Individual wealth is neither a right nor a privilege but a form of stewardship. We are charged, as agents of God, with the duty to guard and protect the world we live in. Our job is to use our money to take care of ourselves and the needs of our families, the community, and all of Israel. This concept has been extended to include all people who are in need.

This is not to say that we should refrain from using the money we have for our own enjoyment or that there is something wrong with us when we do. The Jewish tradition rejects the view that money is the root of all evil. Rather, it teaches us that our relationship to money is linked to the responsibility we have to others; money becomes a potential source for us to do infinite good when we use it to help mitigate the problems around us.

The beauty of this concept is in its absolute equality. No matter how much or how little we possess, or how often we are able to give, each one of us has the potential to consciously become a better person, a holy person, when we use the money we have for the betterment of the world.

KEEPING KOSHER: BRINGING
HOLINESS INTO THE KITCHEN

$\mathcal{S}$ome people mark the stages in their lives by fashion, others by education or career choices. I, on the other hand, can clearly describe my personal evolution over the years to something much more basic. Food, especially Jewish food, has always had a very special hold on me. Whether it was my grandmother's perfect chicken soup, sweetened by adding parsnips to the broth, or my mother's Sephardic eggplant dishes, I have always loved Jewish-style eating and Jewish food.

But to be perfectly honest, I have not been steadfast in my devotion. During my lifetime I have changed gastronomical commitments more often than my hair color.

In my youth I was a serious carnivore, the kind you might see gnawing on the bones of a steak or chicken like a rabid dog. During my college years, I abandoned all meat and animal products in favor of fruits, vegetables and granola. And then there was the tofu thing I did in law school.

So it was understandable that when I called my mother and told her that my family had decided to keep kosher, she reacted as if I had told her we were moving to the third world.

"You're going to do WHAT?" she screamed into the phone. "Don't you have enough to do as it is without adding this to your life?"

I've known my mother long enough to appreciate that her reaction, although couched in a form of mom-hysteria, was really one of love and concern. But I also know that what my mother couldn't possible appreciate is that by creating a kosher home, we weren't trying to make our lives more stressful or difficult. We were hoping to create meaning by elevating the everyday act of eating into something separate, distinct and yes, even holy. By creating a kosher home, we were trying to bring an awareness of the sanctity of all living things to our dinner table.

Where and when did the idea of *kashrut* begin? The concept of restricted foods is first introduced in Genesis when God permits Adam to eat only fruits, vegetables and plants. It was after the flood that Noah was given permission to eat meat. Yet while Noah had no restrictions on which animals he could eat, the Israelites were given a long list of animals, birds and fish they were forbidden to eat when they were given the laws of the Torah. (Leviticus 11:2-30)

Gone from the Jewish menu were animals that did not chew their cud and have split hooves – like camels, pigs, horses, rodents and other wild beasts. Birds of prey such as vultures, eagles, hawks and ravens and all shellfish and fish without fins and scales were also forbidden.

While historically there have been efforts to provide physical, health-related or spiritual reasons for these laws, the Torah makes no attempt to give a rationale for them. They are in a category of laws called *chukkim*, laws which have no readily apparent human rationale or purpose but instead are seen as inscrutable Divine decrees. What we are told is that in following God's law, we will become holy: "You shall sanctify yourselves and be holy, for I am holy." (Leviticus 11:44)

Keeping kosher is a form of discipline that sets us apart as Jews in order to convert the ordinary act of eating into something special and holy. The very detailed laws which include regulations about the separation of milk from meat and proper way animals should be raised, treated, slaughtered, cleaned and prepared are the result of interpretations of the Biblical commandments by the rabbis of the Talmud.

I appreciate how overwhelming it is to convert a non-kosher kitchen into a kosher one and how hard it is to make the commitment to keep a Kosher home. I still struggle with questions of degree of observance, like how long we should wait after eating chicken before enjoying a dish of ice cream. I have learned from talking with people who keep kosher that it is a very personal commitment and that no two families observe it alike. And it's clear to me why so many Jews are intimidated by the idea of keeping kosher – because it feels like an all-or-nothing proposition and they don't know if they can really make that kind of commitment.

I look to the Torah for guidance and am encouraged by the fact that the laws of kashrut were not given all at once but instead, were given incrementally throughout the Torah. First we were prohibited from boiling a kid in its mother's milk, then from eating the blood of an animal, and finally from eating specific types of animals, birds and fish.

It is possible to view this as a suggestion for those of us who are not ready to fully commit that it is better to begin than not to try at all. Step by step, meal by meal, we can let our commitment evolve over time. By giving up pork and bacon, by avoiding shellfish or by eating milk and meat separately, it is possible to raise our kosher consciousness. And in doing so, we can bring awareness, intention and holiness into our kitchens and our lives.

The Many Faces of Jewish Theft

*M*y career as a criminal began one hot summer afternoon when I was six years old and my mother suggested I help her clean out the closets. I was thrilled at the thought of spending time alone with her, lining the dresser drawers with perfumed tissue paper for her perfectly folded scarves and soft, cashmere sweaters. But as the afternoon wore on, I got bored and looked for something more exciting to do. That's when the trouble began.

From the corner of my eye, I saw it peaking out from underneath the wooden shoe rack; her oversized, I-can-fit-anything-in-it pocketbook, the one that smelled like new leather and coins. I surreptitiously took it into my bedroom and emptied its contents onto my bed. A jumble of treasures tumbled out; a lost earring, an old report card, a misplaced glove and a roll of half-eaten butterscotch lifesavers. But my heart raced when I saw the camel colored wallet bulging with paper bills and coins. I knew at the time it was wrong, but I did it anyway. I took about a dollars worth of change and stashed it behind the ceramic clown on my bookshelf.

Before you indict and convict me, let me explain. More than anything else, I wanted to belong to a group of "cool" older girls on my block called the Goodwin Girls (named after our street, Goodwin Terrace). In my first grade mind, they were incredibly grown-up because they rode two-wheeler bikes, stayed out past dark and played freeze tag with the boys. My excitement as a six-year-old consisted of sitting on the curb in front of my house popping tar bubbles with a stick.

Most of the girls came from big families where money was tight. They scrimped and scraped to come up with the nickel it cost for an ice cream bar whenever the Good Humor Man drove by. Surely, I thought, if I gave them money to buy ice cream or candy, they would let me become a Goodwin Girl.

And it worked. My popularity soared overnight as I doled out the funds I had stolen the day before. But word got out and one of the mothers called my parents and told them I was giving away more money than a bank. I don't remember what was worse, the look of utter disappointment on my mother's face or the spanking my father gave me that night. My response was profound: I developed a lifetime aversion to the smell of leather and promised myself that I would never, ever steal again.

I would like to think that I have made good on that promise, that I have never taken anything since that day that didn't belong to me. But I have learned over the years that there are many forms of stealing and most of them have very little to do with the wrongful taking of money or property.

Most of us are familiar with the Eighth Commandment: "Thou Shall Not Steal." While its meaning may be clear to us, what is less familiar is how expansive the Jewish prohibition against stealing truly is.

Traditional Jewish thought establishes that in addition to outright robbery of money or physical property, stealing can take the form of "robbery of the mind." Theft of the mind (or *gneevat da'at* in Hebrew) is tantamount to taking away a person's true understanding of what is going on around him or her. When we intentionally deceive a person and profit from the deception, either financially, socially or psychologically, we steal his ability to determine the truth of a situation.

Theft of the mind comes in many sizes and shapes. When we defraud a person into believing that we care when we don't, when we make insincere offers to help others or falsely flatter a person to gain an advantage, when we take someone else's ideas and use them as our own, we steal something other than money or property. We steal that person's ability to trust in others.

Theft is also found in the misleading information we give about the products we sell, the services we offer or the skills that we have. It can be as egregious as false advertising practices or as subtle as a disingenuous dinner invitation when you know the person will be out of town.

Many years have passed since my heist on Goodwin Terrace but I have never forgotten the feelings of guilt and shame that accompanied my actions. They still haunt me whenever I am tempted to take credit for an idea that is not mine or give a compliment I don't truly mean.

OH WHAT A TANGLED WEB WE WEAVE....

J came home from work earlier than usual because I felt the first signs of the flu coming on. I walked into the house feeling shaky and feverish, only to be bombarded with hugs by my seven-year-old daughter, Lauren.

"Mommeeeeeeeee!" she screamed with glee. "You're home early. Can we play dress-up before dinner?"

"Not now, honey. I don't feel very well. I'm going to lie down and get under the covers. You can come in and I'll read to you in bed, if you want," I responded feeling weaker by the minute.

We weren't more than half way through *Where the Wild Things Are* when the phone rang. Lauren picked it up and started chatting away. It was my mother.

"Oh hi mom," I said with forced cheeriness. "No, everything's fine. I came home early to spend some special time with Lauren." I looked over at my daughter who had a confused look on her face.

After I hung up, Lauren didn't say anything to me for a while. I continued reading until she asked in a whisper, "Mommy, why did you lie to grandma?"

"Oh boy," I thought sheepishly, "I've been busted by my seven-year-old. How do I answer this one?"

"Well, you see honey, I didn't want to worry grandma and I knew that if I told her I was sick, she would get really concerned and call me twenty times a day until I was feeling better. So I told her a "white lie," that's something that isn't really the whole truth but it doesn't really hurt the person not to know so it's okay, you know what I mean?" I asked, exhaling in one long breath.

"Can I not tell YOU something when I think you'll get worried?" she asked demurely.

"Well...," I stammered, aware that by now I was in some pretty muddy waters, "you're still young and its not a good idea to keep things from me or daddy because there's still a lot you don't know and we won't be too worried, even if you think we will, so you can always tell us everything."

"Okay" she said, and to my great relief, jumped off the bed and went into her room to play.

That conversation, and others like it, have bothered me for years. How can I consider myself a good parent and an honest, moral person if I tacitly condone lying in my own home – to my own mother!

There is both wisdom and consolation in the writings of the Talmudic sages who tackled the topic of lying with diplomacy and a deep understanding of human nature when they wrote: "Great is peace, seeing that for its sake even God modified the truth." (Yevamot 65b)

This passage refers to a story from Genesis when God, not wanting to hurt Abraham's feelings or create strife in his home, hid the fact that Sarah laughed and referred to Abraham as an old man when she was told that she would have a baby in her old age.

Judaism considers truth an important value but it does not consider it an absolute one. It recognizes that there will be times when other values in the Torah take priority over telling the whole truth. So was I right when I didn't tell my mother the truth? Does Jewish law condone lying under those circumstances?

Jewish tradition allows us to tell a lie, when not under oath, for three main reasons: in order to save a life, to create peace between people and to preserve harmony within the home or between a husband and wife. The answer is further refined in the Talmud, which gives three other reasons that one may alter the truth: "In the following three matters, learned men do conceal the truth: In matters of tractate, bed and hospitality." (Baba Metzia, 23b-24a)

This text has been construed to mean that "white lies" can be told in order not to brag about oneself or make another person feel less worthy, in order to maintain privacy about personal and intimate matters and to avoid causing harm to or hurting another person.

While none of the above specifically addresses what happened with my mother, I like to think that by not causing her unnecessary concern about my health, I avoided causing her harm. And although I will always feel uncomfortable when I tell a half-truth, especially in front of my children, I know that life will present continuing situations where I will deem it necessary to do so. About that, I cannot lie.

LIFE LESSONS SHARED OVER A LATTE

I had coffee with an old friend this week, someone I've known since I moved to Tucson 28 years ago, when I worked nights as a waitress to support my daytime tanning habit. Over the past three decades, we have sailed in and out of each others lives with an uncanny sense of timing and need. We are not close in the way everyday friends are, but our shared sense of history and abiding love for one another has sustained us through long periods of absence.

As I looked into her face I saw a reflection of how much we had both changed. Laugh lines emanate from our eyes now, sunscreen and Retina A cover our once smooth, sunburned noses and cheeks, and masses of freckles cover our arms, the ones we both work so hard at to keep tight and firm. External changes, all of them, which pale in comparison to the deeper, internal ones that have slowly but steadily altered the way we view ourselves, our families and our place in the world.

"You know," she told me, "I used to care so much more about what people thought of me. I wanted to fit in, to be accepted as part of the group. These days I just want to be true to what I value, to honor the things that are most important in my life – like my family, my work and my friends."

The answer to the question "What is most important in life?" is different for each of us. It is not a static answer but an evolving one, reflecting our changing needs and realities as well as our cognitive and emotional abilities. It is born from an emerging awareness of what gives our life meaning and purpose, what makes us feel that we are truly engaged in the act of living.

What matters most changes depending upon the ages and stages of life that we are in. To a small child, it might range from a beloved pet to a family member, special blanket or birthday celebration. During adolescence, it is related to things of social significance such as friendships, popularity, personal appearance, good times, clothes or music. In adulthood, the spectrum of what is most important widens to include family, meaningful relationships, education, career, wealth, community, spirituality and the future. In the senior years, closeness to family and friends, good health, security, enjoying the present and finding meaning from simply living life often becomes most important.

Obviously these are generalizations which don't apply to everyone. But they make us aware of an important point: that we need to stay attuned to what IS most important to us throughout our lives. Because it is through our continuing awareness of what matters most that we are inspired to act, respond and grow into the individuals we hope to become.

We don't always have the luxury of choosing how we spend our time; yet no matter how busy we are we can still honor what is most important to us in the way we lead our lives; in how we speak to and treat others, how we use the money and time we have and how we show others that we care.

The Hasidic Rebbe Zusha used to say: "When I die and come before the heavenly court, if they ask me, 'Zusha, why were you not as great as Abraham?' I will not be afraid. I will say that I was not born with Abraham's intellectual capabilities. And if they ask me, 'Zusha, why were you not like Moses?' I will say that I did not have Moses' leadership abilities. But when they ask me, 'Zusha, why were you not like Zusha?' for that I will have no answer."

Struggles in the Workplace

I sat across from Jim, opposing counsel in a complicated commercial case, while the court reporter diligently typed the stream of words pouring from my client's lips. The deposition had gone on all morning and my client, exhausted from the intensity of the inquiry, had become a little cranky and loose-lipped. My stomach rumbled like distant thunder and I asked if we could take a recess until after lunch.

"I can't break now. I only have this afternoon to depose your client and the witness. Maybe your caseload is lighter than mine, but I don't have the time to chit-chat the noon hour away." Jim's voice filled the room with unnecessary rancor.

"I just thought it was a good time to break, seeing as we've been at it for four hours and need some food and time to regroup," I responded evenly.

"Your needs are of no concern," was his acid retort.

Okay, you say. He was being a jerk, plain and simple. But at that moment I had to decide how to respond to his tone and implications, balancing my obligation to remain professional and dignified with my baser desire to kick him under the table.

That's when I did a quick mental checklist of what might really be going on. Was Jim so stressed and overworked that time for a sandwich seemed like a day at the beach? Was he worried about the case and felt that if we broke the momentum he might lose the chance to wear my client down? Had I offended him in some way without knowing it?

I began to speculate about who Jim was as a person, not just as the overworked, high-strung lawyer I knew him to be, but as a man who might be trying too hard to play the game without realizing what he was giving up in the process. The room grew still and the court reporter looked nervously at me for a response.

Five words came to mind, words that I had never applied to my law practice before. The words came out of nowhere (actually they come from the Book of Genesis when God created humanity) and weren't what you'd expect I'd be thinking, given the situation. Rather than "See you in court, buddy" or "No need to be hostile," the five words that helped me respond to Jim were: "in the image of God."

In Hebrew, *B'Tzelem Elohim* means "in the likeness or image of God." That humanity was created not only as the highest form of life on earth but in the image of the Creator is a lofty concept to be sure. One that I first understood the morning my son was born and my husband gently handed him to me, still wet and matted from birth. I looked into his eyes and knew at that moment that I was looking into the eyes of God.

Being created in the image of God tells us a great deal about who we are and who we can become. It teaches us that just as God has immeasurable power and capability for creativity, so do we have limitless potential to develop ourselves if we put our minds to it. It teaches us that just as God is infinite and unique, so are we of infinite value and worth. It reminds us that just as God acts with compassion and love towards the people of Israel but also feels great frustration and anger towards them, so should we strive for compassion with others even though we have feelings that confuse, anger or frighten us.

I looked over at Jim and tried to look beyond his patently disagreeable surface to what lay beneath. Maybe he had a bad day, forgot his anniversary or missed a car payment. And as I tried to paint Jim in the image of God, I became aware that my feelings towards him were changing.

"Fine, Jim," I said. "Let's just take ten minutes and order some sandwiches so we can keep going and get through this today."

It didn't take much on my part to dissipate the tension in the room. Jim looked relieved and even a bit sheepish.

How different the world might be if we could recognize that within each one of us, there is something divine, some intangible spark of God-ness, to be honored. For in making the effort to look for the image of God in each other, we might find not only the best in them, but the best in ourselves as well.

BEARING WITNESS TO
EVERYDAY MIRACLES

My husband looked at me like I was crazy but didn't say a word. I lifted my backpack, weighted down with the necessary essentials like food, a sleeping bag and water (as well as some luxury items like gourmet brownies and a bottle of Merlot) and placed it into the trunk of my car. Nothing would deter me from joining my four girlfriends for this Adventure in Nature: Not my bad back, my too-tight hiking boots or my fear of snakes. Nothing!

Hiking this glorious canyon demanded great concentration as we climbed over rocks, slid down boulders and trudged through water. It took us several hours before we reached an ideal spot to camp. Cathedral-like walls of striated granite encircled the sandy spit of beach. We made a fire and shared food and stories over dinner. Waterfalls and desert frogs serenaded us to sleep as we lay in our sleeping bags under a starlit canopy. In the morning my stomach yearned for good coffee while my back screamed for a double dose of Advil. Even so, I felt totally content and at peace.

The solitude of the canyon was remarkable. It had been two days and we hadn't seen a soul or heard anything but running water, frogs and birds. We sang, swam, ate and sunbathed on huge boulders like lizards on a rock. It was as near to perfection as anything I could think of.

Until, on our hike out, Sharon slipped off a steep rock and caught her leg under a fallen tree branch. In a matter of seconds, everything changed. The silence was broken by screams of pain as we stopped short and stared in disbelief and fear. She lay in the water, conscious but unable to move her leg. What were we going to do? How could we carry Sharon out of the canyon when we could barely scramble across the rocks ourselves? How could we get help when the one cell phone we brought in had lost its reception a mile back?

Suddenly, as if in a Lassie movie, we heard the barking of dogs. Within minutes, three large dogs came bounding through the water followed by two young men.

"You haven't seen a doctor anywhere?" I asked half-jokingly.

"Sorry, I haven't," one man replied, but then finished with four words that were magic to our ears. "But I'm a paramedic."

Talk about having a guardian angel. Here, in the middle of nowhere after two days of seeing no one was the answer to our prayers. Jeff was a volunteer paramedic who worked with Search and Rescue, out hiking for the day with his friend Bill. Without a moment's hesitation and with genuine kindness, they became part of our group as if they had been with us from the start. They offered everything from time, body strength and a cell phone (which miraculously worked) to encouragement, humor and emotional support.

We assembled ourselves intuitively, like the inner workings of a clock, each person playing a vital role in our effort to get Sharon out of the canyon. Some cleared the path of branches while others lifted her leg or acted as a brace to hold her up as we slowly and methodically moved her from rock to rock. Separately, none of us could have done it, but together we became like one seamless body with a single mission: to get Sharon safely to a hospital.

Hours later, when the helicopter lifted upwards with Sharon inside, the knot in my throat finally loosened and I tasted the salt of my own tears. I hadn't even realized I was crying. I looked around at my friends, their faces filled with love, concern and relief, and knew without a doubt that what had happened that day was nothing short of a miracle.

I felt the fragility of life, saw it in Sharon's pained face as she waved goodbye from the helicopter. I looked at the scratches on Jeff's arm and the exhausted bodies of my friends and knew, more than ever, how each one of us is so essential and important to all of us as a whole. It was unimportant that our group consisted of Jews, Catholics and Protestants because each of us drew upon our shared compassion, concern, and humanity in acting solely to help another person. It made me realize that it is the human experience that is at the center of all religions, not creed or theological claims. Because it is in the way we act, talk, help, teach, love and work with others, that we stand as witness to the presence of God and the miracles in our life.

GROWING AND LEARNING

JUDAISM IS AN INVITATION TO QUESTION

Recently I had the opportunity to study with a group of interfaith friends, an eclectic group which included Jews, Sufis, Baptists, a Catholic and a follower of Gurdjieff. Our teacher was a liberal Catholic priest and our goal for the morning was to explore the history of Christianity and the development of Christian dogma and rituals – a daunting task made easier by the presence of Starbucks coffee and a box of Krispy Kremes.

We began by introducing ourselves by name, faith and what we hoped to learn from the study session. Since I knew everyone in the group quite well, I was startled to discover something about my non-Jewish friends that I hadn't realized before. Each one expressed deep disappointment or frustration about the religious "ground rules" they had grown up with prohibiting them from questioning the dogmas and creeds of their faiths. As children they were punished for asking simple and honest questions like: Why would a good, moral person who lives in the middle of the jungle and doesn't know about God be doomed to Hell? Or, on the lighter side: If the Bible is a true story then where did all the women in Genesis come from who gave birth to the children?

As I listened to my friends it struck me how differently Judaism approaches the idea of asking questions – about faith, religious beliefs and dogma, even the concept of God itself. Faith and belief are not the starting points of legitimate Jewish living and being; uncertainty and doubt are not signs of religious heresy. Serious skeptics, those who seek meaningful Jewish answers to life's hardest questions are not viewed as second class Jews. Doubt and skepticism are part of being human and Judaism recognizes them as such. As a religion and a way of life, Judaism is designed to reach us where we live, in the trenches of our hearts and our lives, in the midst of our uncertainty, anger, fear and doubt.

One of the first and best examples of the kind of doubt and questioning that is sanctioned in Judaism is found in Genesis 18:25 when Abraham questions God about His decision to destroy the city of Sodom. With a boldness not yet encountered in human history, Abraham challenges God on the basis that there might be some good people living among the wicked by asking: "Shall not the Judge of the earth do justice?"

Even more important than Abraham's compassion towards potentially innocent people is the manner in which he engages God. From the outset, Jewish tradition establishes the right to question God, to build a relationship which permits us to pour out our anger, frustration, fear and sorrow without reprisal or retribution.

Jews are called the Children of Israel, descendants of a man whose name was changed from Jacob to Israel after he wrestled with an angel and refused to release him until the angel blessed him as follows: "Your name shall no longer be Jacob, but Israel, for you have wrestled with God and men and have prevailed." (Genesis 32:28-9)

The word Israel in Hebrew (*Yisrael*) means "to struggle with God." It is our name and our legacy to struggle in our relationship with God in order to build a life of meaning.

Our starting point is the Torah, the central Jewish document which is the heritage of the Jewish people and the foremost book about man's understanding of and encounter with God. However we understand the Torah, whether we believe it is the Divine Revelation of God or the inspired writings of man, we can be certain that struggling with questions about the nature of God, about suffering and evil, and about why we should follow the commandments (*mitzvot*) are all legitimate Jewish questions.

Throughout Jewish history, the obligation to question the meaning of sacred texts has served to strengthen, rather than weaken, our understanding of Jewish law and ritual observance. The Talmud is a wonderful example of how the process of questioning, debating and reconciling theological differences can result in a deeper and more practical understanding of the meaning of the Torah. Filled with legal rulings, legends, homilies and parables it is like a continuous conversation and debate spanning more than 400 years between the rabbis, and testifies to the concept that "There are seventy faces of the Torah."

My friends and I shared a wonderful morning, asking questions about Christian dogma and rituals in an open and accepting environment. While I learned a great deal about the teachings of the Church, I also learned how much I appreciate being part of a tradition that encourages, even requires, me to seriously question the issues that will make me a more committed Jew and a more caring human being.

So Many Teachers, So Little Time

*A*s a child, I always dreaded going to Hebrew School. Although it was only a few blocks from my public school, the lonely bike ride felt like miles as I watched my friends walk away in the opposite direction, arms linked together like a gum chain. Being Jewish in the small town in which I grew up meant being different. It meant missing school in September for a holiday where I was hungry all day long and not having a Christmas tree or colored lights on our house during the dark month of December. And being different was the very last thing I wanted to be as an emerging adolescent.

"How come your Jewish books open up backwards and have those funny-looking letters in them?" Cheryl asked me one day.

"Why do you have to go to school *after* school?" Are you stupid or something?" Linda asked, giving me elbow digs that went deeper than the surface.

I didn't have the words or the convictions back then to explain what it took me years to appreciate; that an essential part of being Jewish is the continuing responsibility to learn, study, and grow throughout our lifetime.

To learn: from our sacred texts such as the Torah, Talmud and hundreds of other works by Jewish sages, rabbis, philosophers and teachers.

To study: alone, in pairs and in groups, with our children, our parents, our partners and our community, so that our decisions and choices in life can be informed by Jewish knowledge, wisdom and practice.

To grow: into a person who is compassionate, caring, respectful, honest and aware of the responsibilities we have to each other, our earth and the Source of creation.

Over the years, my teachers have come in different shapes, sizes, ages, affiliations and sexes. I have learned from rabbis and student rabbis, from cantors and professional educators. I have sat at the feet of great masters from New York to Jerusalem, aware that I was learning from some of the best and brightest minds that modern Jewish thought has produced.

I have also learned from some of the finest people I know, who guided me through the canyons of my curiosity, embarrassment and ignorance and taught me how to love Judaism without even realizing it. My grandmother stands out as one of the greats, a woman with no more than a fifth grade education who taught me how to light Shabbat candles and make chicken soup sweetened with parsnips. My friend Esther, whose generosity of spirit and willingness to share her love of Judaism inspired me to be a better Jew and a better person. My colleague Jeffrey, who patiently explained Hebrew prayers to me, my sister-in-law Judy who helped me keep kosher, my husband Ray, who fought to maintain the Sabbath in a home where weekends looked like whirlwinds.

Jewish tradition recognizes that we encounter many teachers in our lifetime and that it is up to us to take what we can from each. Simeon Ben Zoma, a great Talmudic rabbi answered the question: "Who is wise?" with the following: "He who learns from every person, as it is said: 'From all my teachers I grew wise.'" (Psalms 119:99)

Regardless of whether we study Jewish history or ethics, attend a Jewish cultural series or participate in a Jewish book club, Jewish learning is an integral part of being Jewish. When we commit to Jewish study, we give ourselves the opportunity to learn how Jewish beliefs and traditions can guide us in our daily decisions and help us make sense of the world. Jewish learning is more than a decision to learn about Judaism. It is a pathway to learning about living a more meaningful life.

It has always been hard to set aside the time for Jewish study. That is why the Talmud cautioned us more than 1,500 years ago with the following advice: "Do not say, when I have leisure time I will study, for you may never have leisure time." (Ethics of the Fathers 2:5)

A HEBREW LOVE AFFAIR

I have had a love affair with words ever since I can recall. As a little girl I would whisper words to myself just to hear the sounds of them; magical words like canopy, arithmetic and Ethiopia. As an adult, I have relied upon words as the tools I use to make meaning in my world. In my work, my family, my relationships and my inner life, words accompany me throughout the day, enabling me to bring to life the images, ideas and beliefs that shape who I am.

This is not to say that all words come easily to me. I have never been able to say orangutan without adding a "g" at the end and I still say "head-egg" instead of headache when under stress. And foreign languages really throw me for a loop. My theory in high school Spanish has remained true to this day: if you add an "o" or an "ita" to any English word, the chance is it will *sound* Spanish enough that you will be understood. For example, "Can you help-o me find-ita the school-o?" will definitely lead you to a school, or at the very least, a building with windows.

So you can imagine the excitement I felt when I enrolled in a Hebrew course at the age of 43 at Hebrew University in Jerusalem, ready to conquer the intricacies of a language that had frustrated me since Matt Berman threw eraser tips at me in Hebrew School. I enthusiastically entered the class only to find a room of lethargic college students, most of whom were more interested in rock concerts and bar-hopping than verb conjugation and tenses.

I became obsessed with learning Hebrew, spending every hour of the day – in the classroom, on the streets, at home, even in my sleep – trying to speak the language. I was brazen and I was shameless. I insisted on speaking Hebrew to anyone and everyone who would listen, including a group of Japanese-speaking tourists who wanted directions to the Israel Museum.

Some people never leave home without a credit card; I never left home without my Hebrew-English dictionary. Such determination and diligence, while hastening my comprehension and ability to speak, came with a price. I became a walking, talking malaprop in Hebrew, the originator of more bloopers than Jerusalem has synagogues.

My family's first dining experience in Jerusalem began the parade of horribles. I proudly requested the menu in Hebrew and began ordering more food than we could possibly eat in a week. I was quite pleased with myself until my son asked for some ice for his drink.

"No problem," I said confidently turning to our middle-aged waiter, a man with absolutely no hair and a wide, open smile.

"Sir, may I have some ice please?" I asked in my finest Hebrew.

He looked startled, then hurt as he scurried off. My Hebrew radar detector indicated immediate distress. What could I have possibly done to insult this gentle soul?

When a new waiter came to deliver the food, I knew I was in trouble. Slipping away from our table on the pretext of finding the bathroom, I headed straight for the dictionary hidden in my purse. It was on those worn pages that I discovered the error of my ways.

The trouble was that the Hebrew word for ice and the Hebrew word for bald are almost identical. I had told our unsuspecting waiter that I wanted him – and I wanted him bald! My embarrassment was knee-deep. I was desperate to make amends and returned to the table with renewed faith that I could set things right. I motioned to our hairless waiter and with a smile as big as Montana, asked for a *masrek*. Now he wasn't wounded but outraged. An Israeli called out, "She means a *masleg*, not a *masrek*! This time I had asked the poor guy for a comb instead of a fork!

I might have thrown in the Hebrew towel if there hadn't been a breakthrough one Friday evening at the synagogue we attended. After several months, I still hadn't noticed much change in my ability to understand the Hebrew prayers I said. Even though I knew them by heart, they were really just words I recited in order to be a part of the synagogue community.

Slowly I felt it, like a soft shiver running through my soul. I realized that for the first time in my life I actually understood the meaning of the Hebrew words of *Yedid Nefesh*, the prayer we say to welcome the Sabbath. I heard the passion, understood the poetry, clung to the description of love between man and God which are found within it. No longer were these words mere sounds; they were Hebrew words I understood because I had made them my own.

Hot tears rolled down my cheeks when we began to sing the *Shema* and I understood for the very first time the words that I had recited by memory my entire life. The *Shema* itself is a commandment to hear, to listen, and to understand. I realized that in my efforts to learn Hebrew I had gained much more than mere knowledge of the aleph-bet. In learning Hebrew I had enabled myself to understand the true meaning of Jewish prayers and to make those prayers my own.

Placing a Fence around the Fence

I was seven years old when Joey Schneider died. I knew him for only a short while, but images of the fun we had on his farm chasing after chickens, running through fields of thigh-high daisies, and building a fort by the big pond ran though my mind like a home movie. It was a humid August night at the end of summer when my mother came into my bedroom and told me the sad news.

"Joey died today. He fell in the pond and drowned."

After the funeral, we went to dinner at the Red Coach Diner. Even though I ordered my favorite vanilla malted milkshake, I couldn't drink it. Just thinking of my friend Joey floating face down in all those weeds made me sick.

"It's such a shame, so unnecessary," my mother practically choked out the words.

"If only they had built a fence to keep the kids safe and away from danger" my father replied.

A fence to keep us safe. Those words haunt me still.

When I think of a fence, I envision it as a structure designed to enclose and protect or mark a boundary. Traditional Jewish thought however, expands the meaning of a fence into an important religious principle that is unknown to most of us.

In the opening verse of Ethics of the Fathers, a tractate of the Talmud concerned with moral advice and ethical behavior, the rabbis wrote: "Make a fence (about the laws) of the Torah." Why a fence? Why not a gate leading into it or a wide-open field around it?

The answer lies in the rabbis' understanding of human nature. They appreciated that it would be difficult for us to follow God's laws and that we would easily be lured to stray from them. As a result, they built in many precautions or "fences" in order to safeguard against the temptation of violating the laws of the greatest Fence of all, the Torah.

The "fence around the Fence" idea works in much the same way as our efforts at protecting our children from the hazards of the world. For example, when we teach our teenagers to drive a car, we teach them the rules of the road and how to steer, stop and park. But we also put up additional fences when we tell them not to drive while talking on a cell phone, fussing with the radio or under the influence of alcohol. We add these extra restrictions to reduce the distractions that often lead to car accidents and death in order to keep our children safe.

In Jewish law, some of the best examples of the fence around the Fence relate to observing the Sabbath, the day we are commanded to refrain from all work and rejuvenate ourselves through prayer, study, and relaxation. The Talmud defines 39 categories of work from which we must refrain, most relating to the building of the Temple in Jerusalem. Because making a fire on the Sabbath is one of the prohibited categories of work, we are not permitted to even touch matches since it might lead to making a fire. Because repairing something that is broken is also prohibited work, we may not play music because it might lead to the need to fix the instrument, should it break while we are playing it.

I never had much of an appreciation for the Sabbath laws until my adult years. I couldn't relate to the myriad of religious restrictions that seemed unrelated to my ability to simply relax and enjoy myself. But as my life became more hectic and the pull of home, family, work and community got greater, I realized that I needed more help in letting go of the numerous responsibilities and chores that summon me all week long.

That's exactly why the rabbis created the fence around the Fence. Not because they wanted to tie us down with unnecessary rules and restrictions but because they knew how difficult it is to stop our work and carve out a time of rest. The extra fences are not meant to be roadblocks to spirituality but rather, to assist us in our efforts to renew our bodies and spirit.

There is danger however, in building too broad or too high a fence – causing us to lose sight of what we are trying to protect. An example of this is found in the following story from Genesis.

When God placed Adam in the Garden of Eden, He told Adam that he could not eat from the Tree of Knowledge but when the snake asked Eve about it, she quoted God as saying: "You shall not eat of it *or touch it* lest you die." (Genesis 3:3) According to tradition, this embellishment gave the snake a chance to trick Eve because when he pushed her into the Tree and she didn't die, she no longer believed that she would die if she ate the fruit. Eve's fence was excessive and the results, banishment from the Garden of Eden, were disastrous. From this the rabbis caution us that: "We ought not to make the fence more essential than the principle injunction, lest it give way and destroy the sprouts." (Bereshit Rabbah 19:3)

Jewish tradition teaches us that the fence is meant to keep us safe, in body and soul, by providing additional safeguards to ensure the preservation of Jewish law. The fence is also there to remind us not to lose sight of what is most important in our lives, and not to get lost in the periphery.

JEWISH GIVING:
WHEN IS ENOUGH, ENOUGH?

*T*he clock read 8:21 a.m. in the women's locker room at the gym where I had just finished working out. I had less than 10 minutes to make it to my first meeting of the day. My breathing matched that of a runner as I sprinted towards the locker room exit.

"Could you help me please?" she asked from the wheelchair positioned next to the door. "I need someone to take off my shoes and put on my sneakers and socks."

My body continued at a full runner's pace as my heart stopped short in its tracks. I turned around and faced her, feeling my body tense up in response. Doris (I learned her name from the medical locket she wore) was in her mid-forties and told me, in speech that was thick and slurred, that she'd had a stroke which left both of her legs and her right arm paralyzed.

I know this seems horrible, callous and cruel but for at least five seconds I actually considered telling her that I was already late for work and she'd have to ask someone else for help. The fact that I, a healthy, energetic and privileged woman, hesitated for even one second in my response to help her made me feel guilty and ashamed. I changed her socks and shoes, chatted with her for a while, and then left the gym more than a half-hour late – my mind plagued by a number of questions.

How much and how often should I consciously give to others? Do I have an obligation, moral or otherwise, to do whatever is asked of me if I am capable? Do I have to give more than what feels "good" or "right"? And what if by giving, I compromise my own position so that I become needy myself?

I sought counsel, as I often do, in the wisdom of the Jewish tradition. In Hebrew the word for charity is *tzedakah* which comes from the word *tzedek,* which means righteousness or justice. Judaism views *tzedakah* not as an option but as a mandate, one of the 613 Biblical commandments which God gave the Jewish people.

In the Book of Deuteronomy we read: "If ... there is a needy person among you ... do not harden your heart and shut your hand against your needy kinsman. Rather, you must open your hand and lend him sufficient for whatever he needs." (15:7-8)

Tzedakah is an obligation which arises out of the human responsibility to distribute a part of what we have to take care of others who are less fortunate. This obligation begins within our own home and family and extends out into the community and the world at large. It is based on the idea that individual wealth is neither a right nor a privilege but a form of stewardship for which we are charged, as agents of God, to protect the world in which we live.

According to Maimonides, the 12th century Spanish philosopher, codifier and physician, there are eight levels of *tzedakah.* Going from the lowest form of giving to the highest, they are: 1. those who give grudgingly or with regret; 2. those who give cheerfully but less than they should; 3. those who give only after being asked; 4. those who give without being asked; 5. when the receiver knows the donor but the donor doesn't know the receiver; 6. when the donor knows the receiver but the receiver doesn't know the donor; 7. when neither the donor nor the receiver know one another; and 8. those who assist others by giving a gift or a loan that enables them to become independent.

Jewish law is fairly specific in its answer to the question of how much we should give. Ideally, we are expected to give what is needed to restore a poor person to his former position. If a man has lost all of his clothing in a fire, we should help him purchase suitable clothes. If he has lost his job, we are obligated to provide him with employment either directly or indirectly by helping him find work.

Yet Jewish law is both practical and realistic in its demands, for while it requires us to give the needy what they lack, it does not require us to make them rich or to become poor ourselves as a result of giving. The question remains, how much giving is enough giving? Maimonides answered this by providing us with specific parameters: Ideally, we should give as much as 20 percent of our possessions although the average acceptable gift is 10 percent. Although each one of us has different resources, property and income at our disposal, the obligation of *tzedakah* applies to everyone. Even a poor person who receives *tzedakah* is obligated to give to others.

I learned a lot from the time I spent with Doris – mostly, that in overcoming my more selfish instincts when I stopped to help her, I gained as much from the giving as she did from the help I gave. I felt good about myself and the few moments we had shared and somehow, being on time for the meeting didn't seem as important after all.

Everything I Learned in College, and Then Some

When I was in high school, I did everything I could to distance myself from my Judaism. It wasn't intentional really, or at least that's what I told myself. I was "searching" for my true identity, trying to find meaning in a world where lip gloss and football games dominated the high school scene and being Jewish was definitely NOT "in."

Oddly enough, I turned to every other religion but Judaism in my quest for understanding. I spent nights studying the New Testament with my friends at a local Christian coffee house and joined a Unitarian peace group that protested against apartheid and the Vietnam War. I read books like Siddhartha and started writing poetry, a la Kahil Gibran. I thought the answer to all my problems, from prom anxiety to world peace, was Universal Everything. Unity of purpose, unity of thought, unity of peoples, unity of faith. I became so convinced of this that I even invited my rabbi to a Bahai fireside meeting, to which he graciously declined.

"I respect and honor all faiths," he assured me. "But I cannot join you there until you know more about your own religion and understand that much of what you seek elsewhere can be found in your own backyard."

I was disappointed in his Wizard of Oz response but let it drop. After all, he was the rabbi.

And he was right. For in my first year of college in a comparative religion class, I encountered Jewish philosophers like Mendelssohn, Buber and Heschel; great Jewish thinkers who challenged me to reflect more, experience more and do more as a Jew. And as I began to explore and unravel the ideas that make Judaism what it is, I saw its beauty and wisdom – not just in its uniformity with other faiths but in its unique differences. I became aware that what makes Judaism so unique is that it is a religion which is not bound by a single catechism or creed. While we have statements of belief like Maimonides Thirteen Articles of Faith, we do not have a definitive doctrine or dogma that you have to accept in order to be Jewish. Rather, Judaism provides each one of us with a multiplicity of views on every subject, regardless of whether our inquiry is about the existence of God, why bad things happen or what Jews think about abortion or homosexuality. I learned that Judaism is an action-oriented faith – one that elevates deed over creed. How we conduct ourselves in our kitchens, classrooms, boardrooms and businesses, the way we speak to our parents, teachers, children and friends, how we use the money, time and knowledge we have is as important as whether we pray daily, keep Kosher or drive on the Sabbath. As a college girl involved in all kinds of protests to make the world a better place, these revelations helped sweep away the cobwebs of my own Jewish misconceptions and encouraged me to find new ways of living and being Jewish.

Since my college days, I have grown slowly but steadily into my Judaism like a well-worn overcoat. I have shaped its pockets with continuing questions, adjusted its collar to fit my changing needs as I have evolved from a student to attorney, wife and mother. With each age and stage of my life I am able to understand Jewish wisdom and tradition in new ways and it is this evolving appreciation that keeps it vital and meaningful for me. And in my efforts to learn more, I have grappled not only with the meaning of sacred Jewish texts but with the meaning of life itself.

Digging deep into Judaism has enabled me to find significance in the everyday things I do and has helped me live with a sense of purpose which grounds me as a daughter, wife, sister, mother and friend. And with the advent of each Jewish new year, I welcome the continuing opportunities to learn more to help me become a better, more complete person.

LESSONS FROM THE MOUNTAIN TOP

I struggled to locate something familiar – a porch light, a bird house, anything at all, as my husband and I walked through the streets of the mountain village we had come to know and love. Mt. Lemmon, the Arizona treasure where lush forests, cool temperatures and endless hiking trails have given thousands of tourists and a small community of residents enjoyment and relief, had been ravaged by the horrific Aspen fire.

For the past 15 years we have owned a small cabin there which became a sacred retreat for our family and friends. Less than 800 square feet, it holds an abundance of joy and memories of time spent together as a family – playing card games, sitting on the deck listening to birds, taking long walks or just cooking dinner together. Even our kids didn't mind the absence of television or video games; they seemed to sense that our time on the mountain brought out the best in all of us.

I reflexively sucked in my breath as we walked past the rubble, ash, and melted structures where my neighbors used to live. It looked as close to a war zone as anything I'd ever seen and it was hard to believe that just weeks before fields of wildflowers and thick groves of trees had stood upon what now was a blackened, charred earth.

We were given, free of charge, bags of seed and bales of hay to help begin the re-vegetation process. We had so much work to do and so little time to do it in before the monsoon rains would descend and we faced losing even more of our land to erosion.

"Will any of this make a difference?" I wondered skeptically to myself as my family and I donned face masks and cotton gloves and began the exhausting work of dragging heavy bales of hay across the blackened ground to mulch it.

My mind raced with questions as I worked through the

day: Are we seeding it too much or not enough? Should we scatter the seeds or rake them into the ground? Would the rain wash them away or did they need rain in order to sprout? Could we really get this stuff to grow in what looked like uninhabitable soil?

I know this might sound strange, but while I was busy reseeding the land I had grown to love, I couldn't help but think of God and the miracle of creation. So many details, so many checks and balances, so much that could go wrong. Yet the picture of creation we are given in Genesis 1:28 is that of an orderly, intricately designed process, reminiscent of a paint-by-number picture that becomes our world – original and perfect.

Jewish literature abounds with poetry, psalms and prayers extolling the wonders of nature and the diversity and complexity of creation. It is clear from the texts that we were brought into God's world for two specific reasons: to fill the earth and master it and to guard and care for it. Our extraordinary relationship to the world we inhabit places us in a direct partnership with God. God's creation has been left in our care to develop and nurture for all time.

True, we haven't always done a great job keeping up our end of the arrangement. We have destroyed natural habitats in our efforts to build communities. We have drained resources, depleted eco-systems and polluted the air and water in our attempts to industrialize. But there remains things that we *can* do to keep our part of the bargain with God that are easily within our grasp.

On an individual level, we can live consciously and carefully if we recycle, drive more gas efficient cars and conserve the energy, water and natural resources we use. We can take time to teach our children to value nature and respect the natural order of the world around us. And by supporting organizations like the Sierra Club, the Nature Conservancy and the Audubon Society in their conservation efforts, we can pass the earth on to future generations in the hopes that it will be in a condition worthy of their praise. My family felt exhausted but good trying to restore a small part of our mountain. The reward came when we returned two weeks later and signs of new growth were everywhere, offering us hope and the promise of renewal. I looked up at the clear blue sky and the words of Psalm 96 resounded in my ears: "Let the Heavens rejoice and the earth be glad, let the sea and all it contains thunder praise."

Being Jewish is a Journey,
Not a Race

*T*he year was 1982 and the 12 Kilometer Run for Soviet Jewry was attended by thousands of people who cared about their plight. Dressed proudly in my "Free Soviet Jews!" T-shirt and armed with enough water to fill a small swimming pool, I sprinted enthusiastically for the first half-mile or so, waving to friends along the sidelines like a notable in a parade. But it wasn't long before I noticed my breath quickening, my knees hurting and the sad fact that I was falling far behind the faster, more experienced runners, who sped past me without even breaking a sweat.

My husband and I completed the race together in just under an hour, a feat which as far as I was concerned, qualified us for the Olympics. We may have been new at the running game, but the very fact that we finished made us happy and proud. That race taught us Rule Number One for Running: What you lack in experience and speed, you can always make up in determination and staying power.

A race represents different things to different people. For some, it is the possibility of excelling at a sport and surpassing others; for others, it is the challenge of beating a prior personal record or running on a more demanding course. For my husband and me on that chilly December morning, it was a chance to make a powerful political statement about the urgent need to free the Jews in Russia who were being persecuted for their religious beliefs and prohibited from leaving the country. It was a chance for us to let others know that we cared about their freedom because we understood how precious our own freedom was – living openly as Jews in America.

Freedom to be Jewish in America is a right guaranteed to us by the First Amendment of the United States Constitution. It secures for us the right to live as Jews without government interference and guarantees that we can practice our faith without fear of arrest, confiscation of property, or tyranny of spirit. When I was growing up, I learned about the Constitution in school but never connected it to the fact that my family could go to synagogue whenever we wanted or celebrate Jewish holidays without fear of reprisal. And since we did not practice many Jewish customs or rituals, I never really thought about the freedom I had to be Jewish at all.

In our home, my father's idea of keeping kosher was not putting bacon on his cheeseburger. Between my father's reluctance to practice Judaism and my mother's lack of religious training, we muddled through rituals like the Passover Seder, where every other page in our Maxwell House Haggadah was marked "Skip." It wasn't until I was in my teens that I realized that "Skip" wasn't some long lost cousin but rather a directive to expedite the service.

Yet even though we did not keep a traditional Jewish home, there were things in my house that were Jewish to the core. Like the food in our refrigerator. Sour dill pickles in jars as large as paint cans dripped pickle juice onto containers of stuffed cabbage and noodle kugel with raisins. When my friends came over, they were offered seltzer and mandelbread, instead of the traditional milk and vanilla wafers.

Walking through our home, you learned something about my parents that spoke volumes about their sense of being Jewish. Hundreds of books filled our book shelves and lined our walls. Books about world history, art, music, literature, philosophy, finance, and religion. My parents' relationship to Judaism was established by the way they associated being Jewish with a love of learning and their unrelenting insistence that their children get a quality education.

Added to that was the way my parents viewed philanthropy. No gift was too much when they saw a need, but it was always made anonymously. My father refused to let others know the amount he pledged to any campaign, yet he was the first to stand up at a synagogue meeting in October of 1973 to commit his financial support to Israel during the Six Day war, encouraging many of his reluctant friends to do the same.

What I took away from my upbringing was not a familiarity with rituals or blessings but a foundation upon which I have built a Jewish life and home with my own family. My beginnings may have been meager by some standards but they taught me a very important lesson; that being Jewish is not like being in a race. We all begin at different starting points; we all run on different paths and confront challenges along the way. It's not so important *where* we begin but *that* we begin – wherever the place we find ourselves and at whatever age or stage in our life.

Being Jewish is not like being in a race. It is not about getting to the finish line first or faster or with more medals than other runners. Being Jewish is about making the journey, about deciding to find the path and begin to move closer – to ourselves, our family, our traditions, our culture, our ethics, our history, and our people. And when we begin to do so, we can appreciate our unique destiny.

As the noted Jewish scholar and philosopher, Franz Roszenweig once said: "For the modern Jew, observance is no longer a matter of the all or the nothing. One only has to start. Nobody can tell where this beginning will lead."

MATTERS OF LIFE AND DEATH

L'CHAIM! – TO YOUR HEALTH

I had a car accident recently. Nothing too serious but I ended up with lower back pain and headaches. Since I'm not prone to complaining, I did what any normal, self-anointed physician would do: I diagnosed my problem and called my closest friend to ask her what she would do if she had back pain and headaches. Never mind that my husband is a doctor or that I have a fantastic health plan. When it comes to medical problems, I believe that if it is within my power, I should make every effort to heal myself.

Not to digress, but this tendency has become a bit of an issue at home. I admit that I'm prone to seeking the counsel of total strangers (like the woman in line in front of me at K-Mart) when I have medical questions. I willingly accept her advice about what antibiotic my son should take or whether zinc lozenges really work rather than rely on the advice of my doctor – husband or pediatrician. My husband thinks it's a form of disrespect but I attribute it to the fact that my own mother acquired all of her medical advice from a neighbor who sold Johnson and Johnson products for a living.

I was heartened however, to learn that my approach is not unique. In fact, taking responsibility for our health is consistent with the traditional Jewish view that a person is primarily responsible for his or her physical well-being. This obligation to take good care of ourselves is derived from the Biblical text: "But take utmost care (of your body) and watch your soul scrupulously." (Deuteronomy 4:9)

Even more remarkable is the fact that the definition of health in Jewish thought is inherently holistic in that it goes beyond freedom from disease. Concern for the person as a whole – for the body, mind, spirit, psyche and soul is necessary in order to achieve optimum health.

We see this philosophy emerge from the Hebrew words that categorize health. *Breeyut*, which is derived from the root word *barah*, to create, is used to describe the continuing regeneration of the body that is required if we are to maintain good health. Medieval Jewish literature uses the word *shlemut* which is derived from the word *shalem*, or whole. Good health is an ongoing process of establishing and maintaining wholeness within us.

Jewish tradition elevates the act of taking care of ourselves into a religious duty; it is an extension of the way we acknowledge the sanctity of the life that God has given us. Our job is to guard, nurture and care for our body and soul as a steward would protect his most prized possession. As the noted 13th century Jewish scholar Joseph ibn Falaquera said: "A person must care for his body like an artisan cares for his tools. For the body is the instrument through which one serves one's Creator."

How do we properly care for our bodies? Maimonides, the famous 12th century Jewish sage, philosopher and physician to the Sultan of Egypt, listed the following six items as essential for preserving good health:

1. Breathing clean air;
2. Moderating our emotions;
3. Maintaining a proper, balanced diet;
4. Exercising in moderation;
5. Getting sufficient sleep; and
6. Properly eliminating.

Pretty sound advice coming from a man born more than 850 years ago in Medieval Spain!

I do my best to eat well and get sufficient exercise and rest but there will inevitably be times when I get sick. In those moments when I'm self-diagnosing my aches and pains, it helps to think that my concern is ultimately a commitment for living a healthy life – one that is a gift entrusted into my care.

The Jewish Response to Illness

I am not a large woman. The width of my shoulders spans a mere 15 inches across, just about big enough to give a piggy-back ride to a small child. Yet, in the days that followed my daughter's phone call from the emergency room, my shoulders seemed to expand beyond all physiological odds to carry what felt like an unbearable load.

A poet at heart, she had been up on the roof at sunset watching the colors change from pink and gold to deep orange and purple. She lost her footing getting down and in less than ten seconds, her life changed and so did ours.

My response and ability to cope was nourished by many sources. It began with the way my husband reacted to our daughter in the emergency room as she lay perfectly still in pain, afraid that any movement might injure her spinal cord causing paralysis. His tenderness and ability to let his love for her shine through his own fears helped me focus on what was most important in the days ahead. As we grappled with decisions about pre and post surgical matters, medications and the deep sadness of watching our daughter experience so much pain, fear and loss, we stood together thinking of only one thing – how best to love her so that she would get well.

Family and friends huddled around us like a tightly-knit team, offering words of comfort, friendship, encouragement and even humor. But it wasn't just the words or the flowers, books, and food that they brought into our hospital room that lifted our spirits, it was the gift of being supported and strengthened by our community. That we did not have to go through this difficult time alone made all the difference in the world; it literally gave us the energy we needed to keep going even after many nights without sleep.

The Jewish tradition has always paid heed to the deepest of human needs and feelings. One way Judaism responds to important emotions and landmark life events is through the use of rituals, blessings and prayers. Whether in response to the joys of birth, the covenant of marriage or the deep sense of loss caused by sickness and death, Jewish rituals create a pathway to more fully understand, appreciate and grow from our life experiences, especially when we are struggling to make sense of them.

Throughout the time we were in the hospital and after we came home, I saw first hand the almost magical powers that the Jewish commandment of *bikkur holim,* (visiting the sick) can have on a person. My daughter's mood and determination to get well were strengthened daily by the presence of friends and family around her. Visitors helped all of us fight the feelings of isolation and loneliness that accompany most illnesses; their presence was a constant reminder that we were not alone in our crisis. Visitors also brought us love and the continuing hope that all would soon be well again.

One evening we had a nurse who insisted on telling us about her own surgery, complete with a viewing of the scars. I know she meant well and was only trying to bond with my daughter, but it didn't make any of us feel better. In its attempt to be sensitive to how a sick person feels, Jewish law has an extensive list of suggestions to guide people who make sick calls, most of which are concerned with being sensitive to the person who is ill. Simply stated, we are expected to be cheerful, positive and compassionate when visiting someone who is sick.

Along with the visitors came many cards, phone calls, and prayers for a *refuah schlemah,* a complete and speedy recovery. Jewish law demands that whenever we hear that someone is sick, we should offer a prayer on his or her behalf. The shortest prayer in the Torah for healing is the one Moses said when his sister Miriam was sick: "O Lord, please heal her." (Numbers 12:13) A simple but genuine request to be sure, which makes it clear that our own heartfelt prayers are an important part of responding when someone is ill.

The more formal Hebrew prayer for healing is called the *Mi Shebeirach*, which is recited during the Torah service. Rabbis from every congregation called or visited us at the hospital and put Lauren's name on their congregation's *Mi Shebeirach* list so that her name would be read along with others in the prayer to heal those who were ill. I have always believed in the power of communal prayer, that when people come together to pray for peace or good health, energy is created which moves the world in a more positive direction. But I never truly understood the strength and comfort that I would feel from knowing that for one collective moment, a community was praying for the recovery of my own daughter.

I wouldn't wish what happened to my daughter on anyone and I don't believe that it is necessary for us to suffer in order to grow. What I do believe is that given the inevitable challenges of living, raising a family and growing older, it is both comforting and empowering to know how important Jewish traditions and community can be for us if we let them into our lives.

THE ETHICAL WILL: LEAVING A
LEGACY OF LOVE AND VALUES

*M*y father has always been one of my most dependable fans. Sitting proudly on the sidelines of my life, he roots for me regardless of whether I hit a home run or strike out. When I announced on the night of my college graduation that I was going out west "to find myself," he shook his head, calmed my hysterical mother and then drove me straight to a camping store. As he paid for my new down vest and sleeping bag he looked at me and said: "Whatever happens, at least you won't be cold."

Years later when I told him I wanted to leave my law practice to "maybe teach, maybe write," his blessing came in weekly envelopes containing articles from the New York Times about women who succeeded in having multiple careers.

I didn't always feel this way about Dad, though. It's a kind of later-in-life wisdom that I grew into, mostly as a result of trying to raise my own two children. Over the years I have been humbled in the face of my struggles as a parent. Feigning enthusiasm, offering support and keeping my mouth shut when my children make choices that differ from the ones I want them to make is an art form I am still learning. Now with perfect hindsight, I can see that what previously felt like Downright Dad Domination was really his best effort at loving a strong-minded daughter who sidestepped his advice like a rut in the road.

Living in Arizona, I have worked hard to keep in touch with my parents who live in New Jersey. The phone rings and I am heartened each time it is Dad on the line. My annoyance at the fact that he calls at dinner time is softened by the realization that his voice sounds a bit weaker and he can't remember the second reason why he called. I no longer take his questions about whether I've considered refinancing the house, why I don't buy a bigger car or why

I didn't buy the stock he recommended as evidence of his disapproval or disappointment in me. Rather, I see them for what they are and probably always have been; an attempt to leave his imprint in my life and my heart through the transmission of his advice, values and love.

Recently my father was diagnosed with macular degeneration, a progressive eye disease that can result in blindness. Because he still spends hours every day reading the newspaper and financial reports, the thought of losing his sight was simply devastating. But he has accommodated to this new disability with an upbeat attitude, large print texts and a magnifying lens as big as a Frisbee.

He told me about the procedure he would need to stop his eyes from getting worse. I was scared just listening to him describe it and thought he must be, too.

"How do you do it, Dad?" I asked him. "How do you handle the frustration of getting older, the physical aches and pains, the fear of what might be next?"

My father is not a religious man but what followed was his own version of an ethical will. An ethical will is a lovely Jewish custom, the origins of which date back to the patriarch Jacob. In its simplest form it is a transmission of the values, life lessons and wisdom a parent wants to pass on to a child before he dies.

Unlike a legal will which disposes of property and possessions and must comply with state law, an ethical will bequeaths one's innermost spiritual estate and has no formal requirements. Traditionally, it is written in letterform and can be written at any time during one's life. Some ethical wills are more like continuing letters, added to at various stages of life such as a child's Bar Mitzvah, graduation from college, marriage or birth of a child. Others are written once, later in life, incorporating the important values and life lessons a parent wants to impart.

My Dad answered my question with words that I will carry with me throughout my life.

"Living is all in the attitude," he began. "You never know what will happen to you, what problems, disappointments or losses will come your way. You can't control what happens to you but the one thing you can control is *your attitude* about what happens. You just have to accept, adjust and move on if you want to live life to the fullest."

I thought about the years Dad had struggled with colitis, about the time his business was robbed, about the night he learned his best friend had been lying to him. The inevitability of life's disappointments never changed his way of responding to them. His strength came from his conviction that he would find a way to live with life's curveballs and his power came from his determination and optimism to forge ahead and find meaning in even the most difficult of situations.

"Besides," he added with humor, "now that I can't see so well, my problems don't look so bad!"

Thanks Dad. I'll remember that.

Living With Death: An Inspiring Commitment to Friendship

$\mathcal{B}$y her own account, my mother is not a religious woman. She does not read the Bible, know Hebrew or put much stock in the observance of Jewish rituals. She has been known to comment on my own degree of commitment to Judaism in anxious, hushed tones, the kind she uses when someone in our family is seriously ill. My brother once told me she told him about the "weird tent with hanging fruit" in our backyard (our Sukkah) and the cleaning frenzy I engage in before Passover as evidence that I've gone off the deep end and joined some bizarre cult.

So it was with both amazement and awe that I recently witnessed her response to the painful and inevitable death of her closest and oldest friend, Eleanor, from cancer. For in those long six months, she met the task of loving and caring for Eleanor with instincts and behavior that are deeply Jewish.

She knew from the start how to provide comfort care, the kind that in its early stages took the form of a pot of chicken soup and a brisket big enough to feed the neighborhood but sadly ended with the stroking of a barely conscious forehead covered in sweat. She understood intuitively that visiting the sick, or *bikkur holim*, often meant sitting quietly by Eleanor's bedside, asking nothing, just giving her friend the sense that she didn't have to bear her sickness alone. And she helped create *shalom bayit*, a calm presence in the house, through her hugs and advice when Eleanor's adult children became stressed and argumentative over what to do for their dying mother.

We talked often during this time about the questions that plagued her; theological questions that became real through the process of participating in the last stages of life of her dearest friend.

Why did Eleanor have to suffer so much? Who should be the one to determine the time of her death: the doctor, her family, Eleanor, God? What words of comfort could she speak to her dying friend about the significance of her life, about the children and grandchildren she would leave behind? We covered much more territory than simply pondering those questions. Talking about Eleanor gave me a chance to find out more about my mother – her values, her needs and concerns, her own fears of death. It was a gift that Eleanor gave to us, a time to talk safely in the third person about a very first person matter.

The Talmud, the sacred Jewish text that interprets the Torah, says that when a person meets his death, he will be asked these questions:

"Did you conduct yourself honestly in your business?

Did you take time to study the Torah?

Did you busy yourself with having children?

Did you think about the World-to-Come?"

This text is instructive in that it establishes that the first question we are asked upon our deaths is not "Did you believe in God?" or "Did you perform all of the Jewish commandments?" but rather "Did you act ethically in your business life, in the way you treated your employees and in the manner in which you served your clients and patrons?"

The heart of Judaism is found in Jewish ethics, in the way we treat others in our daily lives. While numerous qualities such as justice, mercy, righteousness, compassion and loving kindness are highly esteemed, at the core of Jewish ethical living is the demand for human decency. It is as simple and as difficult as that.

Jewish tradition does not limit the domain of religious observance nor does it consider the performance of Jewish ritual as superior or more "religious" than the manner in which we live out each day. Praying three times a day is

considered equally as important as visiting a sick friend or
not saying something hurtful about someone you know.

My mother may not be considered a religious person
by certain standards. But in loving and caring for her
friend, she responded in the only way she knew how, from
her heart. And in this act, she confirmed her essence as a
spiritual being engaged in a deeply human experience.

THE MOURNER'S KADDISH:
AFFIRMING LOVE IN THE FACE OF DEATH

I arrived in Tucson on July 4, 1976, *Erev* Bi-Centennial for those of us who are prone to turning a national holiday into a Jewish one. It was hotter than I had ever known but the thought of spending my afternoons poolside, working on my post-college tan, cooled me down. That first night as I watched the evening sky turn from cloudless blue to blazing coral to deep lavender, I knew I had come to the right place.

I stayed with my Aunt Gen who owned a beautiful Airedale dog named Torah. She wasn't much into Judaism and when I asked why she had named him after the Jewish Bible she just shook her head and laughed.

"I named him after one of my favorite movies about the attack on Pearl Harbor called Tora!Tora!Tora!" she said through her laughter. I could see we both had a lot to learn from each other.

We shared so much that summer, my aunt and I. She was lonely, having become a widow less than a year before, and I was full of energy and raring to go. Whenever she hesitated about going to the movies or out for a hike, I pushed her through the door and said, "JUST DO IT!" And inevitably, we did.

We would joke sometimes about how we were the original Odd Couple. I was "religious" and deeply involved in exploring Jewish rituals and traditions; she was a thoroughbred atheist who had no use or respect for anything Biblical. I began to see that, like my father, she was highly critical and suspicious of traditional Judaism. Both of them were first generation Americans who had concluded that the Judaism practiced by their parents was outdated and artificial and offered little in the way of contemporary thinking or being. Nonetheless, Aunt Gen and I shared a "live and let live" philosophy and she never objected to the candles I lit on Friday night as long as they enhanced her dining room when guests arrived for dinner.

"I grew up here," I'm fond of saying. Not in the birth-to-toddler-to-adolescent sense, but in the way you grow up and into yourself after leaving home. Aunt Gen became a second mother to me and I became the daughter she never had. We experienced each other openly and honestly, sometimes as friends, sometimes as relatives but always with great love and admiration for one another. It was a relationship we both needed and treasured.

Aunt Gen was diagnosed with stage IV cancer in January of 1996. They said she had four to six months to live, barely enough time to plan a trip let alone finish what she needed to before she died. We didn't acknowledge what we both knew was true, that every passing day brought us closer to her end. But we cherished those six months because they gave us time and permission to talk – about us, the family, her successes and regrets, about what she would miss most when she was gone.

I asked her once when we were sitting on her back porch whether she believed in God. It was a windy day in March, and the scarf that covered her fragile hairless scalp blew softly around her face. In that one moment, she looked so young I couldn't believe she wouldn't be here to watch my children grow up.

"I really don't think I believe in God," she answered, "but sometimes I wish I did. People are my religion, I believe in the goodness of mankind and the creativity and love of the human soul."

We sat there for a while and then she asked me if I would do her a favor.

"Would you say Kaddish for me after I'm gone?" Coming from a woman who had never once acknowledged that Jewish ritual was important to her, the question stunned me.

"Of course I will, but why?" What I was really thinking was: "Why do you want me to say the traditional Jewish mourner's prayer when you don't believe in religion or God?" She answered as if she had heard my silent question. "Because I don't know for certain whether God exists and I don't want to die without being remembered in the way that my parents were remembered before me. Besides," she added with a grin, "girls can say it now, can't they?"

She was referring to the fact that throughout Jewish history only men had the obligation to recite Kaddish for a deceased parent, a view that has changed over the years in contemporary Jewish movements.

The Kaddish, an Aramaic prayer that is more than 2000 years old, is a prayer that consoles, elevates and renews hope in the mourner that God's goodness will prevail. It is recited at the burial and for eleven months after the death of a parent at daily, Sabbath and festival services. It is a prayer that affirms our awareness of holiness and life in the face of great loss. It makes no reference to death however, only to life and Divine greatness.

My Aunt Gen's experience of God came through the love she had towards the people who touched her life and whose lives she touched. Since her death I have come to understand an essential lesson about life. Love doesn't die, only people do. In asking me to recite Kaddish for her, she affirmed her life and the lives of the people who loved her.

WHO IS AMY HIRSHBERG LEDERMAN?

 Amy Hirshberg Lederman is a nationally syndicated columnist and freelance writer, Jewish educator, public speaker, and attorney. She practiced law for 14 years before pursuing her passion of Jewish education. She has served as the Assistant North American Director of the Florence Melton Adult Mini-School and the Director of the Department of Jewish Education and Identity for the Jewish Federation of Southern Arizona. She currently teaches courses on Jewish spirituality, ethics, law and literature.

Amy received her Bachelor of Arts degree from Oberlin College, her Juris Doctor from the University of Arizona and her Master's Degree in Jewish Education from the Spertus College of Jewish Studies. In 1997, Amy and her family moved to Israel for a year where she studied with an international group of Jewish educators at the Melton Center for Jewish Education at Hebrew University.

Amy has presented at numerous conferences, Jewish Federation events, synagogue, Hillel and Hebrew Day School retreats throughout the United States. She has a nationally syndicated column featured in more than a dozen Jewish newspapers, has published stories in *Chicken Soup for the Jewish Soul* and *Being Jewish* magazine and is a contributor to the *Jewish World Review*. She speaks with humor, passion and clarity and is able to inspire and empower her audiences using her knowledge of Torah, rabbinic and contemporary law.

Amy is available to work with communities in areas of leadership development, community building and Jewish education. Current speaking topics include, but are not limited to:

- Finding the Leader Within: Jewish Models of Leadership
- Honor Your Parents, Teach Your Children: Building Healthier Jewish Families
- Lech Lecha: The Jewish Search for Meaning and Purpose in our Lives
- Chicken Soup and Candlesticks: Creating Meaningful Jewish Rituals for Home and Family
- Women of Valor: Who Are We Now?
- The Ethical Will: Creating a Legacy of Love and Values
- My Grandmother's Candlesticks: Passing the Flame from One Generation to the Next
- The Buck Stops Here: Finding Spirituality in the Workplace
- Jewish Ethics for Ethical Jews
- Fascinating Jewish Trials: Compelling Cases of our Times
- From Moses to Me: Building a Community of Lay Leadership
- If You Know Grapes, Make Wine: Creating Work That You Love

FOR MORE INFORMATION ABOUT HAVING AMY
SPEAK IN YOUR COMMUNITY CONTACT HER AT:
www.amyhirshberglederman.com
Email: amy@amyhirshberglederman.com
Phone: (520) 790-2879 • Fax (520) 207-0510

ABOUT THE ARTIST

*G*ail T. Roberts is more than the artist who created the painting on the cover of this book.  She is one of my oldest and dearest friends and a spiritual companion who has introduced me to people, places and ideas that have changed my very being. I owe to her a lifetime of gratitude for loving me in every stage of life and for knowing that a hippy doctor from Los Angeles would turn out to be my soul mate. I cannot imagine my life without her.

The creation and publication of this book has been a wonderful journey and the thrill of collaborating with Gail on the artwork only increased the pleasure. I have provided information about Gail so that you may contact her if you would like to see more of her artwork.

This is what Gail Roberts says about her art:

"My current artwork represents a synthesis of almost thirty years of artistic exploration. During my career, I have been a professional studio potter, painter, teacher, director of an art studio and a public artist. I continue to welcome new approaches, embrace challenges and enjoy stretching the creative process to new levels.

'Whimsical' and 'bold' are the two most often used words to describe my artwork. Objects or vignettes seen in every day life are able to be reinterpreted with a unique, often humorous perspective. Rich colors display a spirit that is imaginative, playful and sensitive. Through my art, I hope to bring pleasure, humor and light to the viewer.

If you would like to contact me about my art, you can reach me at: Gailarts@cox.net."

ORDER ADDITIONAL COPIES
TODAY TO SHARE WITH
FAMILY AND FRIENDS

Name: _____

Address _____

City _____ State _____ Zip _____

Telephone: _____

Email address: _____

Send your completed order form with check or money
order made payable to Aliyah Publishing to:
Aliyah Publishing, 5425 E. Broadway Blvd. PMB #242,
Tucson, AZ 85711-3704

Or order online at www.amyhirshberglederman.com

Or call: 520-790-2879

Or fax: 520-207-0510

	Quantity	x	Price	=	Total
To Life!	_____		$17.95		$_____
10% discount for orders of 10 or more					(-)_____
Subtotal					$_____
Sales tax: Arizona only, add 7.6%					$_____
Shipping: U.S.: $4.00 for first book, $2.00 for each additional book					$_____
TOTAL					$_____

Thank you for your order!

NOTES

Notes